'Everyone can relate to F**k It.'
THE TIMES – SATURDAY REVIEW

'Self-help for the time-poor and psycho-babble intolerant.'
MARIE CLAIRE

'"F**k It". I was practising the words. They rolled around my head. We need to say "F**k It" when we're out of sync with the natural world; it helps us go with the flow.'
THE OBSERVER

'Stressed, angry or upset? Then try F**k It therapy.'
SUNDAY TIMES STYLE MAGAZINE

'John combines Wayne Hemingway's style with Eddie Izzard's flights of surrealism.'
THE GUARDIAN

'This year, dare to say F**k It... I did it. I relaxed, let go, told the truth, did what made me happy and accepted everyone... I don't feel like a martyr and I had real fun.'
RED MAGAZINE

'The perfect book to help.'
NOW MAGAZINE

'Something making you unhappy? One man's F**k It therapy teaches us to let go.'
METRO

f**k it

Also by John C. Parkin

F**k It Therapy: The Profane Way to Profound Happiness

f**k it
the ultimate spiritual way

John C. Parkin

HAY HOUSE, INC.
Carlsbad, California • New York City
London • Sydney • Johannesburg
Vancouver • New Delhi

Published and distributed in the United States by: Hay House, Inc.: www.
hayhouse.com® • **Published and distributed in Australia by:** Hay House
Australia Pty. Ltd.: www.hayhouse.com.au • **Published and distributed
in the United Kingdom by:** Hay House UK, Ltd.: www.hayhouse.co.uk •
Published and distributed in the Republic of South Africa by: Hay House
SA (Pty), Ltd.: www.hayhouse.co.za • **Distributed in Canada by:** Raincoast
Books: www.raincoast.com • **Published in India by:** Hay House Publishers
India: www.hayhouse.co.in

Cover design: Andrea Amadio • *Interior images:* 232–233 © Michelangelo
Gratton/Getty Images; 234–235 © Shutterstock

The author of this book does not dispense medical advice or prescribe
the use of any technique as a form of treatment for physical, emotional,
or medical problems without the advice of a physician, either directly or
indirectly. The intent of the author is only to offer information of a general
nature to help you in your quest for emotional and spiritual well-being.
In the event you use any of the information in this book for yourself, the
author and the publisher assume no responsibility for your actions.

Library of Congress Control Number: 2013957901

ISBN: 978-1-4019-4599-2

10 9 8 7

1st edition (revised), March 2014

Printed in the United States of America

Dedicated to Leone and Arco,
my boys, and my 'F**k It' models on this Earth
(though don't you dare say that word, boys)

CONTENTS

ACKNOWLEDGEMENTS

A list of names will follow. If I've missed anyone obvious, it's either a) because of my terrible memory or b) because your contribution wasn't as great as you thought it was.

But first, my main acknowledgement is to Gaia, my beautiful wife. We started teaching our F**k It Retreats together in 2005, so much of what's written in this book has sprouted from what we explored together in those weeks, and in our daily lives. Thanks, Gaia, for everything.

Now, here's the list. Thanks for your help in getting this together, directly or indirectly (in alphabetical order, in case you're wondering):

Andrea Amadio, Barefoot Doctor, Peter Baynham, Richard Bolton, Alison Bowditch, Antoine Bowes, Kate Brockhurst, Dan Brule, Anthea Bull, Axel Chaldecott, Bob Coleman, Simon Confino, Dad, Chelsey Fox, Claire Gillman, Lucy Greeves, Karl Grunick, Bisong Guo, John Hegarty, Steve Henry, Rupert Howell, Jont, Armando Iannucci, Jen Lincoln, Patrick Lucocq, Adam Lury, Chris Madden, Mum, Sue Okell, Tony Parsons, Murray Partridge, Ian Priest, Rach, Roi Robertson, Saul, Mark Seabright, James Spence, Alex Wipperfurth, Marc Wisbey.

To the team at Hay House, you're brilliant.

To Gaia, for the illustrations.

To Maria Christofi, for her TCM advice.

To everyone who's shared a F**k It Retreat with us.

To everyone whose surname begins with a 'P'. We rock.

FOREWORD (NEW EDITION)

In his very special book *The Beautiful Life*, former Anglican vicar Simon Parke writes: 'You have been running on a treadmill for so long, but you have decided to step off. And now you are walking across the grass towards the edge of a great cliff, to leap into a gorgeous void. After so much meaningless and exhausting activity – for meaningless activity is particularly exhausting – you long to throw yourself into the strange holding of nothing. Will you dare? The ego is running after you, telling you not to be so stupid, that you'd be mad to jump, to stay on the treadmill at all costs. He says you will kill yourself if you jump. He says there's nothing there. He asks how can you wish for nothing when the treadmill works so well? What do you say? What do you do?'

I answered that question back in 2007, while I too was an Anglican vicar, and this is what I said: 'Fuck It, Mark – jump!'

To cut a long story short, I paid a visit to my boss (the Bishop) after deciding to say, 'Fuck It, I'm going to let him see the real me for once – warts and all.' The result: I lost my job, my home, my income, my place in the community, my security and more. But it was not all loss, for I gained my freedom, my authenticity, my true vocation, my inner happiness and my life as it should be.

To say Fuck It when there seems to be so much to lose, or so great a risk, or so far to fall if it all goes wrong, takes enormous courage. To say Fuck It is not so much to hurl offensive language at 'them out there', but to face yourself (or at least your own ego). The Tao (Way) of Fuck It is to face our own fears and say, 'I'm not going to hold *me* back any more.' To say Fuck It costs, yet the rewards are often far greater than the losses. Fuck It is tough, but necessary if you want to be the person you were meant to be.

And so I applaud this wonderful book by John C. Parkin, and I'm deeply honoured that he invited me to write a foreword for this new edition, especially bearing in mind that I am a Christian priest and thus, in a sense, represent one of the most 'in need of Fuck It' institutions in the world.

Yet the irony is that my own faith (and don't worry, I am not one of those sour-faced killjoys who thinks my religion's the only true one and needs forcing down everyone else's throat) is based on a man who said Fuck It.

Jesus said Fuck It in so many ways. He said Fuck It to the ones who thought women should be kept in their place, and even allowed a woman of the night to kiss his feet. He said Fuck It to the ones who saw booze and feasting as sinful, and even made more wine for an already pissed-up party. He said Fuck It to the ones who saw themselves as righteous and holier than thou, and even stopped them taking out their projected hatred on another. He said Fuck It to the ones who saw religion as something to make them feel superior, and even lifted the fallen, broken and downtrodden into the arms of Divine LOVE. And he said Fuck It to his own personal security and bravely challenged the system, knowing where it would all end. Yes, my own religion is based on Fuck It, yet it has been replaced with perfectionistic respectability.

I think that religious/spiritual people probably need this lesson more than any. We need to get back to the place of the founders of our various paths – the men and women who taught how to live fully and abundantly, listening not to the shallow voices of the surface but to the deep wisdom of the inner voice.

I've often seen the human mind as being in almost permanent dialogue with itself. It's as if there are many voices simultaneously shouting for attention, and most of them are of the ego. However, under them is another voice, quieter yet wiser. Fuck It allows that deeper voice to speak, and helps us to courageously confront the other whining voices by saying 'yes' to the risk, the facing of the fear, the stepping out in faith, the leaping into the chasm, the jumping from the treadmills of our self-expectations.

Anyway, Fuck It, that's enough of my voice. Suffice it to say that you're in for a real treat. So make yourself comfortable, and get ready to never be the same again.

The Reverend M. Townsend
Author of *Diary of a Heretic* and
Jesus Through Pagan Eyes

FOREWORD
(ORIGINAL EDITION)

Fuck It, I'm just going to write whatever comes into my head. I was deliberating about it – wanting to do the best possible foreword because the book fully deserves one, and getting all intellectually prissy about it – when all at once, I stopped and realized what I was doing: a foreword to a book with the bold and irreverent title *F**k It*. So why deliberate?

The keys to liberation are universal and essentially simple: disengage from all the stories you've been telling yourself about life and who you are or should be as you negotiate your way through, and all at once you know yourself as divine, all-powerful, unstoppable and magnificent, as any divine, all-powerful, unstoppable being would.

To do this requires a willingness to relax and let go, not just once but again and again, because the part of your mind that's addicted to and identifies with those stories is a wily fox and will fight for its habit at every turn.

To let go requires a command given to your mind, one that the mind can identify with and which elicits a spontaneous sense of freedom. And what better command than 'Fuck It', for in the instant of uttering these profanely eloquent words you are at one with every rebel who ever lived, with all the world's great liberators, with every maverick who ever bucked the trend. You are free – and in your freedom you are naturally magnificent.

John and I are kindred spirits – I am utterly inspired by him and his brilliant book – I believe it's a major contribution to the human race.

Barefoot Doctor

THE
FOREPLAY

A TASTE: SAY F**K IT TO SOMETHING *NOW*

When you say F**k It, you let go of your hold on something – usually something that's causing you pain.

When you say F**k It, you give in to the flow of life – you stop doing what you don't want to do, you finally do what you've always wanted to do and you stop listening to people and listen to yourself.

When you say F**k It, you carry out a spiritual act (the ultimate one, actually) because you give up, let go, stop resisting and relax back into the natural flow of life itself (otherwise known as the Tao, God, etc.).

When you say F**k It, you stop worrying (generally), give up wanting (mainly) and end up being darn happy to be yourself in the present moment (if you're lucky).

So, before we jump, arm-in-arm, into this swimming pool of F**k It wisdom, have a go yourself now. Say F**k It to something. It could be something small (take a trip to the fridge and gobble down that cheesecake) or big (take a trip to that lazy pig of a fella you call your partner and tell him to take a walk).

Say F**k It to something… anything. And feel the freedom and release that it brings. Multiply that by the power of 10 – imagine feeling like that for most of the time – and you have an idea of what you're getting into.

And, last thing before we jump then, let's SHOUT together: Fuuuucccckkkkkkkk liiitttttttttttttttttt!

A MESSAGE FROM THE AUTHOR

This whole book is a message from the author, of course, but this is the author's message convoy, sending out a bike ahead to meet you, and to prepare you for the arrival of the message proper.

So the man on the bike pulls off his helmet (oohh, matron). And is giggling. Once he's pulled himself together he tells you why he was laughing.

This message will reach you in a (mostly) light-hearted format. Things are usually easier to swallow and digest that way, after all. As Mary Poppins said, 'A spoonful of sugar helps the medicine go down.' Especially when the spoonful of medicine/sugar you're about to ingest takes the flavour of anything you want: which was strawberry for Michael and 'Mmm, rum punch' for Mary Poppins.

So choose your flavour and I'll try to oblige.

The thing is that the whole message is about non-seriousness. So the medicine itself is 100 per cent sugar (with, of course, the E number for the flavour of your choice).

For all of us, life is made up of things that matter. Our value system is simply the things in the world that we've chosen to matter to us (or been handed by 'conditioning'). And the things that matter to us are the things that we take seriously.

When we say F**k It (and we usually do say it when the things that matter to us have gone tits-up), we recognize that the thing that mattered to us doesn't matter so much. In other words – through whatever unfortunate circumstance – we stop taking seriously something that we usually take very seriously indeed.

Things mattering is seriousness. Things not mattering is the land of laughter and lightness.

When we say F**k It, we stop taking things so seriously.

By now, your brain might be buzzing around like a fly in a shoe box taunted by the odours of rotting meat, because the possibility that things might not matter, well, it does your head in. But for most of us, there's also the irresistible perfume of freedom when we find that things might not matter so much after all.

Pause.

For about seven years.

Because that, dear reader, was the original 'Message from the Author' that I wrote for the first edition of this book.

And here I am again, sitting in roughly the same place, revisiting all these words for this revised and updated edition. So, before I tell you some more about the world of F**k It, I thought I'd quickly give you the backstory to how it all came about:

2002: Having said F**k It to careers and life in London, we (me, my wife, Gaia, and our one-year-old twins) go on the road in a camper van and head for Italy (Gaia's Italian), looking for a place to set up a retreat. We find a huge wooded hill with two abandoned houses on it (which we later renovate), near Urbino in Le Marche.

2004: We open the retreat, The Hill That Breathes. It's exciting, it's tiring, and it's a blast. Towards the end of that year, we find ourselves advising our guests – who have come to relax and let go – that it's probably best to say 'F**k It' to the things that are stressing them out. People seem to like this idea; they tell us so and we have a thought: why not teach a 'F**k It Week'.

Summer 2005: Our first F**k It Week is a sell-out success. We find we have lots to say about how saying F**k It can work in our lives to create relaxation and freedom.

Autumn 2005: I write an early draft of this book.

Throughout 2006: I continue to work on the book; I write new chapters; I take chapters out; I start to share print-outs of some of the chapters with guests at the retreat. They say I should publish it.

July 2007: I publish the book myself, printing 1,000 copies. People really love it. Word spreads quickly – including to my favourite publisher, Hay House. I'm talking about them to a mate when I get an email from Michelle Pilley, the UK boss. She wants to talk. I meet Michelle and the team, and we get on really well. They offer to publish the book the following year.

October 2008: Hay House publishes F**k It: The Ultimate Spiritual Way in the UK. It attracts lots of press and is featured on TV's The Graham Norton Show. We are off.

(As I write this, five years later, the F**k It books have been translated into 22 languages and have sold an estimated 400,000 copies around the world.)

2009: We release The Way of F**k It (again with Hay House), a fun little book with lines of F**k It wisdom and illustrations from Gaia.

2011: Gaia and I realize that, while we love teaching F**k It to people, we don't much love the hotel-running side of things. So we find a way to teach F**k It while allowing other people to look after the hotel side of things. We start running F**k It Retreats from other gorgeous venues around Italy.

2012: We release (yes, again with Hay House) *F**k It Therapy*, a book that examines in depth the therapeutic side of F**k It, and features many of the practices we use during our F**k It Retreats.

September 2013: Today. Now. Me writing this, on our big hill in Italy. In one of those houses that we renovated. But it's no longer a retreat – just our home: ahhhhhh.

A few months back, knowing we were going to produce this new, updated version of *F**k It: The Ultimate Spiritual Way*, I went through the original book, crossing things out, adding and updating bits, and so on. But then I realized something: I've *changed*. (Please don't get me wrong here, I've not changed for the better, or for the worse, but changed I surely have). It was almost as if a different John was editing the original book. And that didn't feel right. I actually started to wonder whether I was reducing the quality of the text; in fact, I'm sure I was.

You see, I wrote this book at a particular time in my life, and with a particular energy. I wrote much of it quickly, early in the morning. I wasn't able to type quickly enough to keep up with all the thoughts that were streaming into my head. And I kind of knew, at the time, that I NEEDED to get it all written down.

At the time I felt so full of a sense of FREEDOM. Whenever I spoke to people about this, they would light up, so I wanted to share this sense of freedom with others – in a book. I also wanted (and don't tell anyone this) to write it down for *myself*, in case that sense of freedom, and my sense of EPIPHANY, faded. I realize now that I'd probably felt a similar sense of freedom only once before in my life: when I finished my A levels and left school, aged 18. I had not enjoyed school; I had not enjoyed having to work so hard. Having put my pen down for the last time in the final exam, I came home and pitched a tent in the garden.

I slept in that tent for weeks. I just sat in that tent, loving being free. I then packed it up and went to Cornwall, in the west of England, where I walked the coastal paths, breathed the sea air and slept in my tent. I ate Cornish pasties and shouted every day into the Cornish coastal breeze: I AM FREEEEEEEE.

For a while, life was good. University was a breeze, as refreshing as the coastal air of that Cornish summer. My sense of freedom lasted. But over the years that followed, it ebbed away. And my health ebbed away, too. I found myself leading the kind of life that many people experience – a meaning-full one – with pleasure balanced by pain, soft times balanced by hard. The relaxed me was always accompanied by the worried me, and I felt the burden of attachments and obligations – the need to be this or that, to get here or there.

I talk about some of those times later in these pages – the times preceding the writing of this book.

Then, when we had our epiphany in late 2004 and 2005, which was led by and fuelled by the use of this bizarrely beautiful profanity – F**k It – an almost overwhelming sense of freedom erupted in me.

By 2005 I was a different John from the John of 2004. I had healed. I was full of energy. I'd suddenly seen that I'd been worrying about so much that didn't matter. I spent most of my time just laughing, giggling and playing. It was a more exuberant experience of freedom than the one I'd had at 18. I wanted to run and shout with joy, and laugh 'til it hurt, and to suck life up for everything it had.

And this book is that John speaking: from the very centre of the life-loving exuberance of Freedom, with a capital 'F', and fuelled by the magic mantra of F**k It, capital F, capital I.

> *The magic mantra 'F**k It': capital F, capital I.*

I was desperate to tell the world about what it's like to be free, and how easy it can be to find Freedom with the assistance of this other F-word.

So, who am I, John of 2013, to go messing with the words of Mr. Free, the John of 2005?

So this is what I did: I went searching for what else John of 2005 had written. And I found plenty – stuff that I felt we didn't have room for in the original book; stuff that I felt people wouldn't really appreciate; stuff that I thought might upset people. But, joy of joys, I loved reading that stuff.

You see, I didn't know, back then, that the book would become so successful. I didn't realize that it would resonate so deeply with so many people. I just wanted to share it. And what I know now is that some of the other stuff I wrote will resonate with people, too.

So this is what I've done. I've left most of the original material intact – there are some small changes, mainly to do with dates (you'll read that 'my boys are now 12' a few times!) – and I've simply added in the extra sections that I recovered. And, just so you know, this is what you'll find as extra material:

Sections that I wrote as part of the original book but later omitted for one reason or another (A Message from Offended of Tunbridge Wells, A Message from our Sponsors, We Say F**k It in the Face of Pain, Even Your Own Mind Will Resist Your Impulse to Say F**k It).

A section that predates the writing of F**k It: The Ultimate Spiritual Way, which I was trying to incorporate into the first draft of the book (The Effect on Your Spirit of Saying F**k It).

Sections that I have written since, and wanted to add (Say F**k It to Fame, Say F**k It to Being Uptight, Say F**k It and Live and Let Live).

So, do enjoy your trip through this book. You're treading a now well-trodden path to freedom. Over the years, we've had hundreds of emails from people who've been helped by this book. We've also had hundreds of people attend our F**k It Retreats (which is where it started, after all).

F**k It has rung bells with people.

F**k It has rung bells with people: it has allowed them to relax, to see things in perspective, to walk out of pain and into freedom. I am always touched by its effect.

John of 2013 is touched, and John of 2005 would be, too.

A MESSAGE FROM OUR SPONSORS

Hi,

We're the friendly people from the businesses around the world that provide you with the things that make your life so meaningful.

Contrary to what the author is about to describe about 'meaning', we'd like to remind you that it's meaning that gives your life, well, meaning.

Looking your best is important, so where would you be without beauty products that remind you you're worth it (thanks, L'Oréal), fine clothes (thanks, H&M) or hair with real bounce (thanks, Wella)?

Financial freedom is important. Where would you be without a credit card, and the real opportunity to realize your dreams (thanks, American Express)? Or the possibility of buying a house and having a generous 30 years to repay the loan (thanks, Barclays bank)?

Being healthy matters, so where would you be without low-fat ice cream (thanks, Häagen-Dazs), diet drinks that also perk you up (thanks, Pepsi) or life-enhancing vitamins that also make your urine look pretty (thanks, Sanatogen)?

And giving yourself a treat is important, too, so thanks goes to Cadbury and Mars, Incorporated, for their delicious sugar and fat concoctions.

Life is a search for meaning, and we're happy to provide the goods for that search. And to charge you handsomely for it.

So remember, Things Matter and Meaning Is Good, especially if they have a price tag attached.

Thank you for listening.

WHY SAYING F**K IT IS A SPIRITUAL ACT

When we say F**k It to things that are really getting to us (the things that are mattering too much), we do carry out a spiritual act. F**k It is the perfect Western expression of the Eastern spiritual ideas of letting go, giving up and relaxing our hold on things (attachments).

Of course, we could argue until the Second Coming (mmm, don't you just love that expression?) about what 'spiritual' actually means. In a broad sense, it's usually defined as the non-material: in whatever non-shape or non-form, but even this doesn't quite do it for me. I can get 'spiritual' feelings from the most material and everyday things. So let's not go too mad on an actual definition — it's enough to say that we probably both get what we're on about when we say 'spiritual'. And — in my experience — whenever we relax deeply and let go, we open ourselves to the spiritual.

When you say F**k It to anything you move from tension and attachment to release and freedom. All philosophies, all religions, all spiritual disciplines offer the same promise: freedom.

With F**k It you move from attachment to freedom.

The problem is that it's a very difficult promise to fulfil.

In fact, any philosophy that could fulfil that promise would be the ultimate philosophy… welcome to the philosophy of F**k It.

The problem for most of us in the Western world — stressed-out, uptight, anxious and controlling as we are — is that we need something with the balls of an expression like F**k It to jerk us into a more relaxed state.

It also has the added advantage that it doesn't involve any of the following:

* Praying
* Chanting
* Meditating
* Wearing sandals

* Singing songs to acoustic guitars

* Developing a belief that you're right and everyone else is wrong

* Killing people

* Eating beans

* Wearing orange

* Stopping yourself doing things that you want to do

* Rules

* Pretending to be happy when you're not

* Saying Amen, unless you really want to.

Amen.

WHY F**K IT HAS SUCH A CHARGE

It contains the word 'Fuck'

A book like this is controversial simply because it contains the word 'Fuck'. Funny, really. First because the philosophy behind it is the truly anarchic thing, not the use of the word itself. But mainly because it takes a long time for a word to lose its power.

The word 'Fuck' is truly beautiful.

It's beautiful because it's slang for having sex. 'Fuck off' is really 'Go and have sex', which is not really an insult, more a good suggestion. 'Fuck you' is really 'Sex with you', which is certainly not an insult, more an invitation. 'Oh, fuck' is really 'Oh, great sex' – which, in your moment of frustration, is not a bad thing to be thinking about.

This one word has the power to shock.

You can kind of understand why this was the case when the word was rarely used, when it was hardly heard in most circles. But in the 1980s and 1990s, it seeped and flowed into the language. It crossed barriers of class, race, and age as the expletive of choice. Its malleability is awesome: so much so that it can be used as *any* part of speech. Look at this:

'I thought, "Fuck me" (verb), the moment she fucking climbed (adverb) out of the fucking car (adjective), I just didn't give a fuck (noun); I mean, like, fuck (conjunction), I had to fucking (adverb) fuck (verb) it (misogynistic use of the impersonal noun and just fucking rude).'

And the remarkable thing is that – even with this virus-like ability to spread – the word has kept a good deal of its power.

Sure, it's now possible to put it on the front cover of a book in a way that wouldn't have been possible 20 years ago, but it's that single word that draws so much attention to the book.

A Message from *Offended of Tunbridge Wells*

Dear Mr. Parkin,

I think it's just disgusting that you've used the F-word in the title of your book. It's people like you who are dragging this country down.

That you then add insult to injury by using the word 'spiritual' next to this abominable word makes me sick to the pit of my stomach.

Being spiritual is nothing to do with the F-word. I've spent 55 years at my local Anglican church, and the F-word has never once been said. In fact, in all my 67 years on God's Earth, I've never once had a F. Not once.

Yours,

Offended of Tunbridge Wells

Dear (Miss) Offended,

You don't know what you're missing.

Even though you're 67, I'd say F-It, and get yourself F'ed smartish.

Yours,

J. C. Parkin

It's all about anarchy

Saying F**k It is like sticking two fingers up to the world of meaning, convention, authority, system, uniformity and order. And this is anarchy. Anarchy literally means 'without a ruler'. And anarchists do propose a state free from rulers and leaders. But the wider meaning of 'anarchy' is the absence of any common standard, purpose or meaning.

And this is the key to the anarchistic heart of F**k It. In life everything supports our relentless pursuit of meaning and the collection of numerous meanings. Even though meanings cause us pain, everything around us supports the process of collecting meaning. In order to live harmoniously together, we try to agree on standards, purposes and meanings.

So anything that threatens some of these collective meanings, the sacred cows of our semantic universes, is a great threat. Anarchism – the actual absence of meaning and purpose – is the greatest threat of all.

The narrower political connotation of anarchism – to overthrow the state – is nothing compared with the disruptive power of its true meaning: to overthrow a common perception of meaning and purpose. In this sense, anarchism is the most disruptive and radical philosophy that mankind could ever dream up.

When you say F**k It, this is where you're going: you're tapping into a philosophy that scares the living daylights out of everyone.

When you say Fk It, you tap into a philosophy that scares the living daylights out of everyone.**

So F**k It is loaded with two types of explosive: the word 'Fuck' itself packs an impressive and offensive punch, and the phrase taps into the philosophy of pure anarchy.

And just before you get scared, stop reading and think, 'I'm not interested in anarchy,' there's an interesting philosophical footnote hidden within the etymology of the word 'anarchy'. *Anarchos* (yes, this is all Greek, by the way) was a description often applied to God – to be 'uncaused' and 'without beginning' was considered divine.

This is a great moment. A moment when whole stadiums (or *stadia* if you know your Latin) of people should stand up and applaud and cheer. Here I am, writing about F**k It being The Ultimate Spiritual Way (which it is, by the way), and arguing that F**k It is in essence true anarchism, when I discover that God – GOD, no less – was referred to as *Anarchos*.

Holy Mother of Jesus, and Father as well, this is good news. Anyone would think there was a God guiding me through the presentation of His Ultimate Philosophy. But hey, God, I'm sorry, the whole concept of You is one commonly held meaning-thing that we anarchically have to say F**k It to.

Sorry, God.

HOW TO READ THIS BOOK

Most of you in the West will read this book from the beginning (front) to the end (back), unless you're one of those people more accustomed to reading celebrity magazines and prefer to flick through something from the back to the front. Just so you know, that won't help you with the ending (it's on the cover, anyway: F**k It is The Ultimate Spiritual Way).

If you're from a country where you naturally read books from the back, have a go, though the words won't make much sense anyway, so it's probably best to wait until the book is translated for you (and I'm looking forward to the various mis-translations of the title, especially 'Sex with It: Find God Through Sex with Inanimate Objects').

But here's another great way to read the book for everyone (West and East): try opening the book randomly and see what turns up. It's like using tarot cards. Who knows how this works – but it does seem to. Have a go now just to confirm this (and surprise yourself). Close the book. Breathe deeply and focus on finding something that you need right now, today. Then open the book randomly. Go on, do it. It's a great way to read. If you do this regularly and keep getting the same page, then it's probably still working: it's me telling you from a distance that you really need to focus on that area of your life.

Another great way to read this book is to read a section, then go out and tell people how much you're enjoying it, and how your life is changing by the minute. In this way you benefit yourself (good karma for spreading the word), others (who benefit from the message) and me (who's using all the proceeds from this book to build a house made of chocolate that I will slowly eat my way through, then claim the full amount on insurance, saying it was termites, and start the whole damn thing again).

I

WHY
WE
SAY
F**K IT

WE SAY F**K IT WHEN WE GIVE UP DOING SOMETHING WE DON'T WANT TO DO

Every week, you clean the windows. You do it religiously and conscientiously. But you're bored with it now. You do it because your mother always told you that clean windows say a lot about the owner. Someone with dirty windows, she thought, was probably dirty themselves.

But the pain of doing it every week has become so much recently that one Monday you just say, 'F**k It', and watch daytime TV instead, with a packet of chocolate biscuits. It feels great. As the weeks pass, you enjoy seeing the windows getting dirtier. They become a symbol of your new freedom. When it's getting difficult to see through them, you hire a window cleaner. You feel even happier with your new F**k It attitude when he is young and gorgeous… and you fancy bursting open a can of Diet Coke, so to speak.

When the things that we thought mattered to us start to give us pain, we can get to the point where we say F**k It. This is when we stop doing them and do something more fun instead. So:

* We say F**k It to trying to get fit and watch the telly instead.

* We say F**k It to being nice to people we don't like and ignore them instead.

* We say F**k It to getting to work bang on time and try being late instead.

* We say F**k It to the cleaning and get a cleaner instead.

* We say F**k It to God and worship the devil instead.

In fact, we say F**k It whenever we give up anything that is causing us some pain. We may say F**k It and give up being someone we don't want to be. We may say F**k It and simply give up caring about something we thought we should care about.

We say F**k It to all the obligations that we feel: from family, friends, work and society to the whole world out there. The pressure that everyone puts on us to be a certain way, and do certain things, just gets too much occasionally. And we say F**k It and do our own thing.

WE SAY F**K IT WHEN WE FINALLY DO SOMETHING WE DIDN'T THINK WE COULD

So we finally do our own thing. For whatever reason, we stop ourselves from doing lots of things we'd like to because we think we shouldn't.

At this very moment, there are people saying F**k It and:

* finally going over to the boy/girl they fancy and telling them how they feel

* walking out of jobs they've had enough of to travel the world

* finally speaking their mind to a friend or family member

* taking a sickie for the first time in their career

* peeking into the wife's wardrobe and trying on that pretty party number

* speaking loudly in libraries

* eating a whole chocolate cake

* giving another driver the finger, then speeding away

* lying on the grass, just staring at the sky for hours.

This is freedom. Finally doing what you really want. Saying F**k It to the world and what people think of you and going for it.

This is the side of F**k It when you need an accompanying rock soundtrack. This is the stuff of those old Levi's ads: riding into an office on a motorbike, picking up the girl and riding off into the sunset.

WE SAY F**K IT BECAUSE OUR LIVES ARE TOO MEANING-FULL

At the core of any F**k It utterance is our relation to meaning in our lives. The truth is, our lives are too meaning-full. Which is a nice cosmic joke. We tend to think our life's struggle is to find meaning: we want to find meaningful things to do; we worry about the real meaning of life; we worry about the meaningless. Yet it's the accumulation of meanings that causes the very pain that we end up having to say F**k It to.

We stopped cleaning the windows because the pain of cleaning the windows became greater than the meaning we attached to having clean windows (instilled in us by a parent).

We headed out on the highway because the pull of the open road finally overcame the meaningfulness of the structured career, mortgaged house and widescreen TV.

So let's look at the history of meaning (and pain).

How we fill our lives with meaning

Oh shit, look who's just turned up. It's Eamonn Andrews (or Michael Aspel, depending on your age). He's burst into the loo to catch you reading this book… or stepped onto the bus… or leapt out of the wardrobe in your bedroom to say: This Is Your Life.

So up you get and make your way out of wherever you are with him. And we cut to the studio full of people from your life and a big screen at the back with a picture of you on it. Then you appear with Eamonn, as if they'd constructed the studio right next door to your house. And we're off: You were born in a suburban semi in 1965 to Jean and Derek Mayhew… etc., etc.

But this is you. So go back to the date *you* were born. And let's join you as you emerge gasping for air from the beautiful, dark warm place where you've been hanging out for the last nine months. What a bloomin' shock… all those bright lights and people… and there's no liquid to float around in; just space, just air.

Here you are. You have entered a space that has no meaning to you whatsoever. And that – at this point – is of no concern to you either. For a while now, you're going to be happy with simple meanings: mother's breast means food and drink and, well, mother's breast means food and drink. All the people gawking at you and making funny noises mean nothing.

The meanings of things grow naturally. And they're normally related to simply whether these things cause us pleasure or pain. The breast is pleasure. Funny feeling in our belly is pain.

Eamonn now turns the page to a picture of you at the age of four; you are playing. Can you remember what it felt like then? Can you remember the pleasure you took in the simplest things? You would watch raindrops fall down a window pane. You'd go outside and look up into the sky and feel the rain on your face. You'd adore the smell of the rain on the dry concrete. Sometimes you'd get an idea that you wanted to go somewhere else or do something else. But generally you'd be happy exactly where you were: immersing yourself in the texture of everything around you.

The meanings of things had developed: lots of things gave you pleasure, and some gave you pain. And you were now pretty conscious of what those things were, to the point where you'd sometimes try to replace some of the painful things with pleasurable ones. And as you flick through the pages of your life now, looking at photos of yourself as a teenager, the natural search for meaning continues.

By now it means something to us to have friends and be liked by people; to have people around that fancy us; to have people around who love us; to be doing well at school or in sport or playing a musical instrument.

And our world of meaning becomes more sophisticated: sometimes it's about just having fun; sometimes it's about other people approving of us; sometimes it's about getting fulfilment from something we're doing; sometimes it's about helping other people.

And as we flick through the pages – through college, through our first job, through relationships, maybe through starting a family – we see the tapestry of meaning that makes up our lives become more and more elaborate. Or, like a scout who accumulates badges on his arm, we slowly but surely add to the list of things that mean something to us.

We *accumulate meanings* like a scout *accumulates badges.*

And this – for most people – is life.

And – most probably – This Is Your Life.

We create a life of things that have meaning for us: things that matter. Or you could say that these things are our values: they are the things that we value in life.

The better an employee we are, the more our job matters to us.

The better a partner we are, the more that relationship matters.

The better a citizen we are, the more other people's welfare matters.

Things matter. And for most of us, things matter big-time.

Everything in society confirms that things should matter… so we never question it. But as we move through life, the list just gets longer and longer. So, as Eamonn rolls his bandwagon of reflection into the present, have a look at what matters to you.

You can probably tick off a good few of the following things that matter:

* how you look: whether you look too fat or too old or too short or too tall

* how successful you are in what you've chosen to do with your life

* the people around you: family, partner, friends

* making a difference with your life: by helping other people or doing something that changes things for the better

* money: simply having enough, or getting to the point where you have a great deal

* getting the bills paid

* having a good holiday every year

* being honest

* doing the right thing whenever you can

* being reliable

* having a laugh

* trying to do something with your life

* God/Buddha/Muhammad, etc.

* your health

* finding your true self

* finding your life purpose

* finding inner peace

* getting to work on time

* meeting deadlines

* setting a good example

* not swearing in front of the children

* not upsetting the apple cart

* speaking your truth

* having time off

* gardening

* music

* keeping up-to-date with the soap/comedy you're currently addicted to

* being there for people when they need you

* having a nice car – or having a car that simply gets you from A to B.

And, of course, we could continue the list forever. Because there are infinite possible meanings in this world… infinite potential for things to matter.

So, for one moment, compare the list you have now with that image of yourself as a four-year-old. Phew, the responsibilities of adult life, eh? Practically without realizing it, you have created for yourself a whole convoy of things that matter.

Burt Reynolds is up front in the truck that really matters most to you. And behind you is every other truck/station wagon/bike of things that matter to you. And this convoy takes one hell of a job to keep on the road. Ten-four.

Life has other ideas

We're cruising down the highway through Arizona, USA. ZZ Top is on full blast. My moustache is fine and masculine. There's a blonde in the seat next to me, and she's wearing 70s hotpants. What more could a man want?

But this convoy is my responsibility. After all, I put it on the road. And no matter how conscientiously Chuck services the vehicles (and the ladies, ahem)… with so many mean machines on the road, there's always the possibility of mechanical disaster.

It may be a flat tire on one of the flat-beds. That slows us down a little but doesn't stop us.

It may be a broken fan belt on one of the pick-ups, but I just purloin some chick's tights to sort that one out. But we have 34 camshafts out there. And 34 hot gasket heads.

Not to mention the injection systems, limited slip differentials and big ends (you should see mine; any mechanical problems there and you'd have a whole load of disappointed honeys).

Then there's the weather. And we get some weather here. Flash floods. Tornadoes. Hailstorms that can kill a man.

Every single thing that matters exposes us to the elements of life.

Our life of things that matter is just like this. Every single thing that matters exposes us to the elements of life. Every thing that matters to us is like having a plan for life that we expect life to stick to.

But life has other ideas.

So no matter how hard we try to stay healthy, we sometimes get sick.

No matter how hard we try to get to work on time, sometimes we get delayed and we're late.

No matter how much we try to do the right thing, sometimes we get drunk and do the wrong thing.

No matter how much we want to be liked, sometimes we're not… no one calls us and we feel terrible.

Sometimes life has other ideas about one of the things that matter to us.

Sometimes life has other ideas about a few of the things that matter.

Sometimes life has other ideas about the whole bloody lot.

The bigger our convoy of things that matter, the more likely it is that life's going to bugger around with our plans for it.

Meaning is pain

Anything that has meaning for us – anything that matters – carries the potential to cause us pain. Meaning is a brightly coloured box with pain inside. And sometimes – without us wanting it to – the lid just bursts open and the pain comes pouring out.

> *Meaning is a brightly coloured box with pain inside.*

The problem is that meaning – things mattering – is attachment. And anything that we're attached to has the potential to turn round and bite us.

The Buddhists do a big thing on attachment. And you can see why. It's their equivalent of sin. Freedom from attachments takes you a good way down the road to total liberation. In fact, it may well be the road itself. And the hard shoulder. And all the Little Chefs along the way. And maybe even the porta-loos in the lay-bys, though I'm not entirely sure about that last bit. That may be pushing it a bit far.

Here's the rub, though – you try dumping your attachments. Dumping all your desires. It's not easy. No, that's like saying running a mile in a record 30 seconds is not easy. There's a darn good chance it's not possible. Ever.

But anyway – on with the argument – I don't want to get you down too much. Not yet, anyway. Enough to say for now that meaning in whatever form is attachment. And attachment carries some form of tension. When meaning goes, the attachment goes. And so does the tension.

Let's take a look at what happens when one meaning or another – one or another thing that matters to us – really starts to cause us pain.

WE SAY F**K IT IN THE FACE OF PAIN

What matters to you right at this moment, more than anything else in the world, is getting to shag Christine, the gorgeous goth you see in your media studies lectures (if you're a woman or a gay man, please imagine Chris, the gorgeous goth you see in your media studies lectures, and adjust the following details accordingly).

Christine does something to you that no one has ever done before. You've read about love being a drug, but this is like no drug you've ever tried. The desire you feel for this woman when you see her black hair, red lips, ample hips and tantalizing, err, hands is like the moment before a nuclear reactor blows, and wipes out all the sheep in Wales for years to come. You are fit to burst and you can't contain it. The desire hurts. When you close your eyes, she's still there. She's in your dreams. You're aching, and it must be down to her because you haven't been to the gym since high school.

You've seen Christine in the bar with a guy called Steve, but it doesn't look serious. Nothing that true love can't wash away as easily as an unexpected mid-summer flash flood will wash away a ramshackle campsite foolishly positioned on a frequently flooding flood plain.

Then, one day, it happens. She sits next to you in the lecture. And you manage to exchange some words. You tell her your name, and she tells you hers – durr, as if you didn't know.

One thing leads to another. Well, actually, this thing only leads to lots of other things like it (for now): you chat in the coffee bar, you chat during the lectures (well, before and after, anyway, as Christine's a very conscientious goth girl and never wants to talk *during* the lecture).

But things are progressing nicely. They say that the best relationships are based on friendship, so this is a good foundation for your relationship with her. Even if there isn't one. Yet.

Then the critical moment comes – a moment that will change the rest of your life.

You're sitting with Christine before the lecture starts, exchanging the usual banter. You're trying not to let her catch you looking at her milky breasts (milky white, not milky milky; she's not lactating, for Christ's sake). And then one of her friends comes in. You've seen them together before, but she doesn't usually attend this lecture.

The friend smiles when she sees you. (Hey, hey, you think, your luck's in. Christine's clearly been talking about you.)

Cheekily, she says to Christine: 'Is this Steve, then?'

And Christine replies: 'What? Are you frickin' serious? Do you really think I would…'

And she stops, and she turns to you. Because she realizes what she's said. And to mix a double, she suddenly realizes how you feel.

But it's too late. The damage has been done. The gun has gone off. And there's no escaping the fact that when you look down, your white T-shirt has a growing red stain right over your heart. You touch your chest. And sure enough, when you look at your hand, it's covered in sticky blood.

No doctor, not even Doctor Who (he's medically trained, you know), can patch up this hole. As you stagger out of the door, you start to choke on the pain of attachment. This gothic black box has burst open and the pain is just flooding out.

Three days later – suitably numbed by a good deal of Red Bull and vodka – you stand in the middle of a pitch-black cemetery (which strikes you as suitably symbolic given the death of your gothic love), stretch out your arms, look up into the heavens and shout:

'Fuuuccckkk Ittttttt!'

After that you feel a good deal better. The goth is dead to you. It's her loss. She matters no more. In this instance, life is a wet leather football on a cold day, and it's just caught you in the balls. At first, the pain is unbearable – you chew wet grass – but then you're off again, trying to score the winner.

And that's what F**k It does. Sometimes things feel as if they're just too painful to bear. And some part of you just gives up caring. The thing that mattered so much, somehow doesn't matter any more. And the freedom that comes from that is a blast and a half.

> *The thing that mattered so much, somehow doesn't matter any more.*

We do it with the little things

You work in a sandwich bar on London's Oxford Street. Your job is to help prepare the food, and though it's not like being a chef in a top restaurant, you take pride in your work and like doing what you do.

So, showing up to work on time and doing a good day's work matter to you. And sitting stationary in a tunnel somewhere between two London Underground stations when you were supposed to start your shift five minutes ago is doing you no good at all.

You've been sitting there for 16 minutes (yes, you know *exactly* how long). The driver's already announced twice that he doesn't know what the problem is, but he assures you that as soon as he does, he'll let you know.

What makes this even more frustrating is that, if you'd known about the delay sooner, you could have got out of the Tube and walked the rest of the way to work. You might have been a couple of minutes late, but it wouldn't have been enough to wind up your boss. Because at this moment, your boss will be looking at her watch, re-checking the rotas, and tutting as she says your name. That's what Emilia is like. She's from Sweden and she's very precise.

As the second hand sweeps slowly round the face of your watch, everything is lateness getting bigger and bigger. You tap your fingers. You tap your foot. You curse. You look around the crowded Tube carriage and everyone is doing the same thing. Tutting, cursing, tapping. And, shit, there's Emilia, up there on Oxford Street, doing – guess what – tutting, cursing and tapping.

But then, like a little bubble bursting inside your brain, you suddenly see yourself as if from the outside. Are you *really* getting this stressed about being half-an-hour late to make some flamin' sandwiches? For Christ's sake… another bubble bursts…

F**k It.

And your whole body relaxes as you slump back into the seat. Your breathing slows down and you look around as if you've seen a vision of the Virgin Mary herself. Everyone looks so stressed and stupid, but you feel so blissful and relaxed.

What are these idiots worrying about? Far worse things are happening to someone on this planet every minute of every day.

Once you say 'F**k It', you'll feel blissful and relaxed.

Chill out, boys and girls. Wake up and smell the bubbles.

You really begin to enjoy this time to yourself; you close your eyes and feel as if you're falling backwards. This is heaven. Perhaps the train actually crashed and the driver is St Peter, informing the passengers that he doesn't know how long it will be before they are cleared to go through the gates of heaven.

You feel the seat beneath you: it is like the comfiest armchair you've ever sat in. Why can't the other passengers feel that? We're so lucky to be treated to such comfortable seats – they would have been wooden benches a few years ago, you know. Let's count our blessings. In fact, you're surprised that people don't come down here, into this cosy rabbit warren of an underground network, just to relax. They should rebrand London Underground as a therapeutic relaxation experience and invite people to descend the long metal escalators to escape the madness of the city above.

Life is good.

And later that day, the people who eat the sandwiches that you have (belatedly) made feel a tiny rush of freedom rising up through their bodies. Like a tiny bubble floating up to the top of their heads and then bursting.

We do it with the big things

Now it's time to change (heads) one more time before we wander off somewhere else for a while.

This time you're Emilia, the precise Swedish manager of the Oxford Street branch of a successful chain of sandwich bars.

You've been working at this central London branch for four years, and you're doing well. You started off serving at the counter of the Stanstead Airport branch, but your talent was soon spotted, and over the years you've been promoted often, finally reaching the heady heights of your current position.

It may not sound much to the media people who swagger into your silver-plated food emporium, but being the manager of one of this company's flagship branches is quite something.

The job is hard, but the money is good, and with this experience on your CV you'll be able to get an amazing job in Sweden's successful healthy snack food equivalent, 'Talem Forum'.

Your job is just about everything to you, in fact. You've recently split up from your boyfriend, who left shouting the rather hurtful, 'Yes, you do look like the blonde one from Abba, but after she's been made up for pantomime to play one of the ugly sisters.' So after work, you tend to head home for an evening of television and a couple of Double Choc Delights.

Now, two days after some early-morning travel chaos resulted in half your staff turning up seriously late for work, you're in a regular catch-up meeting with your immediate boss, Graham, the Central London Shop Director.

Graham is a *very* sweaty man. Even on very cold days, he's a very sweaty man. And today – if that's even possible – he's even sweatier than usual.

'Emilia,' he says, through sweaty lips, 'the bread's not gone mouldy yet, but it isn't that fresh either. It's past its best, if I'm honest. We're looking at flat sales for the Mega Club, yet within this demographic, we should be seeing a 10 per cent increase year-on-year. And your tuna niçoise baguettes have taken a plunge recently, too.

'So, to cut to the quick, to be honest, and to cut a long story short, Emilia, we'd like to give some fresh blood a chance to inject some adrenaline into the engine of this shop. Sorry. But you'll get a month's pay, and you can finish today. We've really appreciated your help, Emilia, but as I say, the granary loaf here is beginning to look a bit too crumbly for our liking. Thanks.'

Two weeks later, you are on a plane to Sweden. At the age of 36, you are going back home to your parents – in failure. Your big plans have ended in nothing. If Talem Forum were going to consider you now, it would only be for a role vacuum-packing preservative-filled sandwiches. You have nothing. And you are nothing. Your relationship has failed. Your career has failed. Your dreams have failed. And here you are, looking at an empty packet of peanuts and the back of a blue leather seat that's far too close to your face to be comfortable.

One solitary tear drips down your cheek.

And then something happens. The tear touches your lip and you taste the salt. And you stick your finger into the empty packet of peanuts to taste that salt. And you inspect the blue leather seat in front of you and then lean forwards to sniff it – the smell reminds you of the new cars that your father had when you were a child.

And you look across the aisle to a man sitting with his head slumped forward. He's around the same age as your father, and you love the cardigan he's wearing. You don't know why, but you love it. It looks comfortable and cosy to you.

Then you glance past the man to his wife, who's reading a gardening magazine. And you suddenly want to garden. You've never gardened in your life, but you want to garden now. You want to plant a seed in moist, dark earth and watch it grow every day. And that's what you'll do when you get home. You'll get up early in the mornings, and you'll plant seeds.

What have you been doing? What have you been worrying about? Sandwich bar manager? F**k It. What a stressful, uptight, miserable existence that was.

What the fuck does it matter? What matters is life.

What the fuck does it matter? What matters is life. And the feeling of carpet under your bare feet, right now, in this cramped, high-altitude space… That's Life… F**k It, this is Life, for God's sake.

Perspective teaches us about meaning

You might remember this from a Bond movie, or maybe from one of those magazines that told us how life would be in the future (and of course, it never has been): picture a man standing upright, holding on to two bars, then taking off and flying around. Jet propulsion for one person. You pull back a lever, open the throttle and you're 100 feet up. Let's call this your Perspective Machine.

We are wandering through the woods of life, looking at the trees. And the trees are all the things that matter to us. Some we like the look of, and we take care of, others fall down right in front of us. Some even fall *on* us. Because things sometimes go seriously wrong. Terrible things do happen to us, or around us. Someone close to us dies; we're involved in an accident; we find out we have a serious illness, and so on.

When these things happen, the Perspective Machine goes flying up through the trees into the sky. And all the things that mattered so much to us, we can hardly see from up here.

People who discover they have cancer suddenly can't understand why they were worrying about so many insignificant things before: the in-tray at work; managing to pay their taxes; the fact that they'd put on weight over the last few years. In one instant, all the things that really mattered so much suddenly matter very little or not at all.

Hanging up there in the Perspective Machine, you can still see the trees down below, but they're now so much smaller. And now that you can see all of the woods and the fields around, you realize those trees are pretty insignificant.

With the news of 9/11, 7/7 or the Asian tsunami, most of us went shooting up in our Perspective Machines. Suddenly all those little things that we'd been so preoccupied with in our lives seemed so pathetically irrelevant. We were alive and our family was alive. And that was all that mattered.

> *Given perspective, all the little things seem pathetically irrelevant.*

Anything that sends our Perspective Machines up into the air – from personal tragedy to world tragedy, to seeing something that really makes us think – is just like saying a big F**k It to all the normal concerns in our lives:

35

'F**k It, what was I worrying about?'

'F**k It, I need to really live and stop getting stuck in these little things.'

'F**k It, I'm going to help people and make a difference.'

Of course, we could also go through a thought process that takes our Perspective Machine up into the stratosphere.

It goes something like this: I am one person among seven billion people on this Earth at the moment. That's one person among 7,000,000,000 people. That's a lot of Wembley Stadiums full of people, and even more double-decker buses (apparently, these are the standard British measurements for size). And we live on a planet that is spinning at 67,000 miles per hour through space, around a sun that is the centre of our solar system (and our solar system is spinning around the centre of the Milky Way at 530,000 miles per hour).

Just our solar system (which is a tiny speck within the entire universe) is very big indeed. If Earth was a peppercorn and Jupiter was a chestnut (the standard American measurements), you'd have to place them 100 metres apart to get a sense of the real distance between us.

And this universe is only one of many. In fact, the chances are that there are many, many more populated Earths – just like ours – in other universes.

And that's just space.

Have a look at time, too. If you're lucky, you may spend 85 years on this Earth. Man has been around for 100,000 years, so you're going to spend just 0.00085 per cent of man's history living on this Earth. And man's stay on Earth has been very short in the context of the age of the Earth (which is 4.5 billion years old): if the Earth had been around for the equivalent of a day (with the Big Bang kicking it all off at midnight), humans didn't turn up until 11.59.58 p.m. That means we've only been around for the last two seconds.

A lifetime is gone in a flash. There are relatively few people on this Earth that were here 100 years ago. Just as you'll be gone (relatively) soon.

So, with just the briefest look at the spatial and temporal context of our lives, we are utterly insignificant. As the Perspective Machine lifts us up so far above the woods that we forget what the word means, we see just one moving light. It is beautiful. A small, gently glowing light. It is a firefly lost somewhere in the cosmos. And a firefly – on Earth – lives for just one night. It glows beautifully, and then goes.

And up there so high in our Perspective Machine we realize that our lives are really just like that of the firefly. Except the air is full of seven billion fireflies. They're glowing beautifully for one night. Then they're gone.

So, F**k It, you might as well REALLY glow.

Fk It, you might as well REALLY glow.**

And there we go again. Did you taste it? That was the brief taste of freedom. Sometimes it doesn't last long. But it's an unforgettable taste.

Personally, I've always tasted it when I've contemplated the utter meaninglessness of my own existence. It's a rush of freedom and it tastes good. If my life means so little, then F**k It, I might as well go for it and just have a laugh.

What happens when the meanings become too much

We're about to take the Perspective Machine so far up into space that it just dissolves, like sugar in a hot cup of tea.

It may never happen to you, but sometimes a life crashes. And it's like one of those spectacular crashes from a 70s thriller, where the car goes straight through a barrier on a corner that happens to be on the steepest slope you've ever seen, and the car smashes against the rocks and crumples up, then bounces down the slope, smashing into more pieces as it goes until it lands in the canyon below, a smashed-up heap. Then there's a pause. Then it bursts into flames.

This could be started by one of the big things that we've talked about before: one of the things that normally give you a good deal of perspective. But these things don't always cause lives to crash. People have kept their equanimity through the most incredible trials and tragedies. But lives do normally crash when some of the things that people have placed a lot of meaning on go very wrong.

But also lives crash for no obvious reason.

When a life crashes, you – and those around you – know about it. It's not a lesson in perspective. It's not a lesson in anything. It's just a deep dark void of despair. It's when people think they're hitting rock-bottom and they just keep going.

I experienced a crash of sorts myself a few years ago. It wasn't so much a smashing-down-the-rocky-slope crash as a serious bump, but it was one of those that will give you whiplash injuries bad enough to keep an osteopath's children at private school for a day a week at least.

Let me set the scene of this everyday collision. We had been wandering around Europe for months in a camper van with barely a care in the world. The summer seemed to last forever. Especially as we were still on the beach and swimming in the Adriatic in southern Italy in late October. But the time came to return to

London and make a few pennies before our next outing (whenever that might be).

We drove into London on the 5th of November. This is usually a day of mild excitement for me, given the prospect of exploding dynamite, writing your own name with sparklers and getting bits of tin foil in your teeth after eating a jacket potato. But within three days we had gone from sun, sea and surf to the dark, drizzly, grizzly streets of south London. That, plus the prospect of having to work, and my rapidly failing health, sent me into a big downer.

The following night we were arguing about how to get a bloody futon out of the van and into our new home, a tiny south London flat, when I lost it. I pulled the camper van across the traffic and came to a halt; half the camper was on the pavement, the other half across a lane of traffic. I got out and just went to lie down in the gutter. Given the considerable amount of rain that was falling every hour, the gutter was more like a river. I lay there and curled up like a little boy and started moaning.

And that was the high point of the week.

For the first time in my life I lost all sense of meaning. I hated being alive. Every single moment I felt in pain. When you're in pain, normally you can escape it in some way. Even if it means taking very strong painkillers. But the horrible dawning truth for me was that this was one pain I could not escape, because it was simply the pain of being alive.

Well, of course there was a way to escape that pain, too… by not being alive. But although I could really understand why people take their own lives, it wasn't something I seriously contemplated.

Gaia was supportive. But for a while I was well beyond help.

We went to a workshop together. She assured me that it would be a 'safe space' to be myself, and for people just to listen. As we were on the Tube, nearing the north London location of the workshop, I started to feel something I'd never felt before. I realized that I was so down… that so little mattered to me… that I really didn't give a shit what anybody thought of me. And this was amazing. I didn't care what the other passengers thought of me as I hung my head and sobbed occasionally.

As we got to the comfortable north London house to join the workshop, I realized I did not give a fetid dingo's kidney what any of these polite people thought of me, either. And this felt very new for a man who *did* care what people thought of him… throughout my life it had mattered to me very much how I was seen.

So I used this safe therapeutic space to the max. In the usual 'share' at the beginning, some people opened up and cried a little. And everyone felt for them, and put an arm round them. And previously in workshops like that I might have cried a little and everyone would feel for me, see me as a man really getting in touch with his feminine side, put an arm round me and give me a hug.

But I blabbed like a baby. No one could touch me. Nothing would help. I was at the centre of a beautiful therapeutic exercise that really should have worked for me. But I was in the same empty, dead and dull space afterwards as I was before. And I learned something about therapeutic groups: the patience for people in a difficult place is not that deep… especially if the therapeutic methods on offer don't seem to have an effect. People were actually getting pissed off with me for being so darn down. And I didn't give a shit about this either.

And I still remember that new feeling I had that day. In the dark despair of the living pain I was feeling, I could also feel a freedom

I had never before experienced in my life: it was the freedom of nothing mattering. In my nihilistic gloom, I was just saying F**k It to everything.

The dark cloud passed and I slowly returned to a 'normal' view of life. But something stayed with me: that feeling that things really didn't matter like they used to. Or rather, I'd lost something that never came back: the feeling that everything matters so darn much.

I realized that things really didn't matter like they used to.

In the following years I read a good deal of spiritual literature. Well, in fact, that's all I read. I read everything I could get my hands on about Taoism, Buddhism, shamanism… and all the colours of New Age spirituality. I read everything from the most influential contemporary teachers. And something started to strike me reading about these modern teachers: that many of them were telling their personal stories and that they were very similar… they were all about the crashes that they'd had in their lives.

So please step forward: Brandon Bays, Eckhart Tolle and Byron Katie.

Brandon Bays – after years of working in the healing field – was devastated when she found she had a large tumour. Yet she achieved an astonishing and rapid self-healing. But 18 months later, she was hit by a series of terrible blows. Her beautiful house in Malibu was burnt to the ground. Then all her income was taken by the IRS, so she had no money in the world. Then her adored daughter Kelley, her 'soul mate', wrote saying she didn't want to have anything to do with her any more.

And, finally, her husband revealed he'd been having a serious relationship with someone else. Bang. In the middle of this, she woke up: time stood still and she decided to trust. She was immediately bathed in a total feeling of love – a feeling that love was everywhere. Brandon Bays 'woke up' and later created the inspiring book, *The Journey*.

Eckhart Tolle lived – until his 30th year – in an almost constant state of anxiety and depression. Then one night –

> *I woke up in the early hours with an absolute feeling of dread. I had woken up with such a feeling many times before, but this time it was more intense than it had ever been… Everything felt so alien, so hostile, and so utterly meaningless that it created in me a deep loathing of the world.*

At that moment, his 'deep longing for annihilation, for non-existence', popped and turned into something else. He had an insight about existence – about the 'self' that he was having trouble living with – that stopped his mind completely. When he came round, his perception of the world was transformed. He saw the beauty in everything and he lived – moment to moment – in peace and bliss. Eckhart Tolle 'woke up' and later created the bestselling work *The Power of Now*.

Over a period of 10 years, Byron Katie's life slowly spiralled down. She descended into depression, rage and paranoia. At times she couldn't leave the house or even bathe or brush her teeth. Her own children would avoid her through fear of her outbursts. Finally, she checked into a halfway house for women with eating disorders. There, she was separated from the other residents because they were frightened of her.

Soon after, as she lay on the floor, she woke up with no concept of who she was. 'There was no me,' she says. She felt only joy and acceptance. When she returned home, everyone thought she was a different person. Byron Katie 'woke up' and later created the beautiful work, *Loving What Is*.

Now, all three ideas/processes have a great deal of merit. But there's something missing, isn't there? Going deep into your emotional layers (*The Journey*) and living more in the now (*The Power of Now*), or asking yourself four questions about what pisses you off (*Loving What Is*) have got diddly-squat to do with what joins the three together:

* They all had major crashes in their lives and then something happened.

* They all said the biggest F**k It they'd ever said and then something changed.

So shouldn't they be teaching that? Shouldn't that be the process?

I know it wouldn't be quite as bestselling, but shouldn't the process really be about having some major crash in your life?

So you've signed up to the Crash Your Life, Say F**k It and Wake Up course. It's cost you £10,000 for the one-month course. Our team of specialists is ready to crash your life:

* Our impersonator calls your boss and pretends to be an employee of a competitor… and claims that you've been passing on confidential information to them for serious cash.

* Our pickpocket has slipped £2,000 in notes into your desk drawer that morning.

* Our Brad Pitt look-alike then starts following your wife and manages to 'accidentally' bump into her. Within three days your wife is called away on a last-minute business conference. And the business, of course, is Brad Pitt-alike.

* Our hacker uses the details you gave for your direct debit to us to hack into your bank account and steal all your money.

* Our identity thief wipes your name from both the deeds of your house and the registration document of your BMW 5-series.

* Our bailiff takes over your house.

* You are now left with (practically) nothing and no one, and as you sit on the curb outside your (ex) house, our martial artist with a hood mugs you and grabs your Rolex.

* At this stage, though we make no guarantees, 78 per cent of clients say F**k It. And five minutes later they wake up.

Job done.

But seriously, this is obviously not something I'd recommend. So don't blame me if you bring on some kind of life-crash and it doesn't work. It means you're just a silly bugger. And if silly buggers ever wake up, they're still silly buggers, so why would you want to go and do that anyway?

What I *do* recommend is using the spiritual process of saying F**k It to start releasing your hold on all those meanings that have the potential to cause you so much pain.

2

ESSENTIAL F**K IT TECHNIQUES

These five techniques will help you to live a F**k It life. In fact, I highly recommend that you tattoo the techniques onto your fingers. That way you won't forget them. Give it a nice flowing typeface – though I wouldn't italicize it or you might end up looking a bit country restaurant.

As you may well soon observe, the techniques flow into one another and depend on one another. Well, that's a bit like making a fist with your tattooed fingers: ready to smash your uptight life into submission.

RELAXING

Most of us don't know how tense we really are. Not you? You're actually really relaxed? OK, let's see.

As you're sitting reading this, begin to focus on your shoulders: you can probably feel them dropping as you relax them. Then move to the neck, feel the tension dissolving away. Then go to your jaw: let the jaw feel slack as you relax it. Then the forehead and the muscles around your eyes.

Now go back to your shoulders. The chances are they've tightened up again: so try to relax them and let them drop once more.

And this is how it works. We find tension where we didn't think there was any, and as soon as we move our attention away, the tension returns. It can be a little disconcerting when you first get into the habit of going into the body consciously like this: because your impression is that you're actually quite tense (whereas before, your ignorance was a peculiar form of bliss).

If you ignore tension in your body, though, it does what children (and some adults) do when they're ignored: it starts shouting, screaming and generally misbehaving. This misbehaviour takes the form of aching necks, headaches, backaches, etc. So have a go at listening to your body *before* it starts to shout for your attention.

Remember that we're very simple beings, too: we tend to try to avoid pain and increase our own pleasure. So far we've been talking about avoiding pain. Try also, then, to find pleasure in relaxing. Try to find as much pleasure in relaxing as you would in a glass of wine, a kiss with your partner or _____ (please insert your favourite pleasurable activity here, though do be a tad careful in case someone else picks up this book after you; I don't want the expression of a pleasurable activity to become, ironically, painful for you).

I call this 'internal pleasure seeking'. Now some smart-arse once pointed out in a workshop I was teaching that *all* pleasure is internal. Well, yes, of course. But I'm talking about finding the source of pleasure inside you rather than outside yourself. This usually wouldn't cross our minds. We desperately try to stimulate internal pleasure (otherwise, yes, known as 'pleasure') through an external search. Again, write the things that tickle your fancy in the margin if you fancy (if we fill this book with too many spaces it will become too much like a workbook and I hate those, or we'll get letters from people saying, 'I bought your book expecting some meaningful advice and all I got was lots of spaces. Next time I'll buy some blank paper from the stationer's: it's a lot cheaper').

If you can find the source of pleasure inside yourself you'll never be bored: you'll be self-sufficient and you'll become a very cheap date, too. But the biggest boon is that if you can find pleasure in the very thing that can boost your own health and lead to a long life, happiness and possible enlightenment, then you're a damn sight more likely to do that thing on a regular basis.

Find the source of pleasure inside yourself and you'll never be bored.

So go on, retire to your room, shut the door and do a bit of internal pleasure seeking. And after you've done that, try to find some really deep pleasure in simply relaxing. Start to enjoy what it's like to take a deep breath. Enjoy the feeling of your hands tingling as they relax more. Get turned on by your whole body feeling as mushy and slushy as ice cream melting on a hot summer's day.

LETTING GO

Maybe it's because we innately know that everything is impermanent that we so desperately cling to it. But cling we do. We know that our youth vanishes, that we and our loved ones will die one day, that whatever we have accumulated can easily be taken away from us, that one day our skills might not be wanted, that a day may come when our love might not be reciprocated. But we go on clinging.

Everywhere we turn we are faced with impermanence. I'm writing this in early October, and as I look outside I'm faced with nature's yearly reminder that everything fades away.

Of course, the more we cling, the more pain we feel as things fade, disappear, or die around us. And sometimes the more we cling, the more these things happen. Imagine someone in a relationship who is, yes, clingy. They hold on to what they think they love with an iron grip, are jealous at the slightest thing, spend their time in fear of what terrible things might happen rather than enjoying the relationship as it is. How does that make the other person feel? How long does that relationship last? (Bad. And not long. Just in case you were sitting there scratching your chin, wondering.)

The key to being able to let go of all the stuff you're holding on to is knowing that you'll be OK if you don't have it. And that's the truth. This is a good exercise: go through all the things that you really want to hang on to in your life – the partner, the job, your health, your sense of humour, your family and friends, the soaps on the telly – and tell yourself that you would (actually) be OK without them. You can survive with very little. And though the passing of people and things can be painful, you will survive.

Though the passing of people and things can be painful, you will survive.

If you're up for it, say this to yourself a few times: 'I am OK with things passing and fading away in my life. I will be OK no matter what happens to me and those around me. I let go of my hold on life and allow life simply to flow around me and through me.' Now light a candle and burn off your own eyebrows. Noooo. Don't just do what I say.

But do relax (finger 1), let go (finger 2) and get ready to accept (finger 3) everything as it is.

ACCEPTING

We're in such a terrible state nowadays. Things really are just getting worse. You can't get on a bus without thinking that it might be blown up by some extremist. And that's if the bus comes. What with the government handing over everything to private companies, who just put money first, there's no one who'll bother with you if there's no money in it. So that's just typical, standing in the rain in the middle of July, waiting for a bus that never comes.

Is it just me, or is it raining more in the summer? It's rubbish, this global warming stuff. It's colder, wetter, just another reason to tell us what to do with our lives. And anyway, if it's getting warmer, why are my gas bills going up? Shouldn't they be going down if we're using less? I rang them up and asked them, and some young chap in India answered. He was very polite but of course had no idea. At least he was polite, that's not something you get here any more. No politeness, no respect.

Do you know how much we moan, here in the UK? Well, I say 'we', I should be saying 'you' as I now live in Italy, where they don't moan much at all (OK, you still get game shows hosted by old men who ogle a stage full of girls in bikinis… Hey, maybe there's a link here… Note to the BBC: bring back 70s game shows with Sir Bruce Forsyth and babes in bikinis… that would stop blokes moaning – for a while at least… As long as you then balance it with a game show hosted by Germaine Greer with loads of beautiful boys in trunks, you'll be fine: then the girls will stop moaning, too).

I notice it even more now that I only surface in Blighty occasionally. You're so uptight and moany. There's always bad news on the television, or people in soaps moaning and shouting at one another, or on *Big Brother* bitching and moaning about each other, and newspapers happy to see that the gorgeous so-and-so is looking a little chubby or too thin. There were endless pieces just this summer about Victoria Beckham being too thin: that she eats just the inside of a banana skin and licks the salt off a crisp every meal. They screamed that she is such a terrible example to all young women. Well, I'm sorry, but isn't she a *great* example to all young women? If you eat less than a small bird with a stomach upset you start to look like a small bird with a stomach upset.

Yes, girls, that woman ain't pretty. She doesn't do it for us boys. Please

Please feel free to chub out a bit.

feel free to chub out a bit, eat lots of ice cream, then you'll get even more of us crossing the dance floor to ask you for a dance… or whatever they do nowadays.

This is why we moan and bitch and criticize: we don't feel too good inside, and we try to find reasons outside ourselves for this discomfort. As you start to feel better inside (by saying F**k It, by relaxing and letting go), you'll get to like that feeling: and you won't find it as easy to moan about everything. After a while you'll positively dislike it because it will make you feel worse, not better.

You'll find that it's best to try to accept things around you just as they are (and this will be easier as you lose the need to justify your own painful feelings). The truth is (I'm sorry to break this to you) that there's usually diddly-squat we can do about most of the things in our lives that piss us off. We can't do a great deal about late buses, terrorists, incompetent politicians taking us into phoney wars, young people swearing and being disrespectful…

Even stuff closer to home: your boss being a bully, your partner being selfish, your children being lazy. Sure, you can leave your job, and your partner, and kick the kids outside to do a bit of good, healthy exercise. But until you're ready to do these things, stop bloody moaning and accept things as they are.

Accepting everything, just as it is, is a beautiful state to get to. Just feel it now: what would it be like to accept yourself just as you are, not slimmer or taller or better looking, just as you are right now? What would it be like to accept your life just as it is: job, family, friends, sex life, prospects, the whole bloomin' lot, just as it is right now? And what would it be like to accept the world – fucked-up, messy, warming up, war-strewn, greed-littered – just as it is?

Try it today. Accept the things that don't go according to plan, the people that don't treat you quite how you'd like to be treated, the bad news as well as the good. Start to enjoy feeling good inside yourself. And remember that you don't need to moan and criticize any more. And if you do feel crap inside (like we all do sometimes) try to accept that feeling, too, without looking for things outside yourself to blame it on.

WATCHING IMPARTIALLY

The Watcher is not some pervert sitting behind drawn curtains, ogling Mrs Tardywells as she unfastens her corset late at night (before flossing seductively by the light of the moon). No, it's what those of us who eat beans for a living call the ability to watch what goes on in your own mind and body impartially. This is sometimes also referred to as 'consciousness' or 'awareness' (both words are used more narrowly by bean-eaters than by philosophers). But let's stick with The Watcher.

Sitting still for a little while (usually off-puttingly referred to as 'meditation') is a good opportunity to get in touch with your inner Watcher. Do you see how giving him/her that capital 'W' has already given him/her some importance in your life? Sit there and, as the thoughts start to roll in – as they invariably will – develop a sense of watching the thoughts (from above if you fancy), as if they're not yours. Don't get involved with the thoughts. Don't judge them. Just accept them. It may help you simply to observe the thoughts in an impartial, non-judging way – e.g. 'Ah, killing the cheating boyfriend with a neatly sharpened axe: OK'; 'Ah, so hungry I could skin my pet tabby and barbecue it for tea: interesting.'

Here's another image for you. You could imagine The Watcher as a CCTV camera on a busy high street. The camera sees everything. It doesn't intervene or shout out, 'Hey, you, big nose, you look ridiculous in that jacket.' It just watches. In fact, the chances are that there's no human being watching a screen of big nose and his jacket. The camera is just a piece of dumb machinery watching (and most probably recording, just in case). A camera watching, not judging or criticizing.

And do you know the effect of this little bit of inanimate machinery? People behave themselves more. And that's pretty much what happens in your mind/body, too. The more you watch impartially – accepting what is seen just for what it is – the better your mind/body is likely to behave. It doesn't have to behave better, of course: there's no MI5/NSA going to be looking at the footage of your thought crimes. But the truth is that when you accept your thoughts and feelings just as they are (through The Watcher), then everything tends to slowly calm down a bit.

Have a go and see for yourself.

And if you're having trouble with it – with getting some distance between you and your thoughts/feelings – have a listen to this. Years ago, we were living in a small flat in London. Every night I would sit cross-legged in silence for half an hour (at around midnight). The flat was part of a huge block, so you could hear the noises of humanity being human at all hours: toilets flushing, doors slamming, TVs blaring, babies crying.

As I settled myself, and my mind began to slow down, I slowly became aware of voices next door. They were male voices, maybe two people, just chatting away about the usual inane day-to-day stuff. I could just about hear what they were saying if I concentrated hard enough. And I remember feeling a little surprised that they were talking like this – so audibly – at this time of night. I listened a little more. I contemplated that I'd never before heard people talking next door: I knew there was a middle-aged man living there alone, but I'd never heard him with anyone else. And I listened.

Then I realized with a jump that the voices weren't next door at all: they were in my own head. I was listening to my own thoughts (as inane and day-to-day as they usually are) as if I were completely separate from them. I tried to tune in again. But the spell had been broken. I was astonished. I really had been convinced that these voices were coming from next door. I understood (maybe for the first time) that I am *more* than my thoughts. I understood that there is something else – in my head, or elsewhere – separate to the thoughts that I'm having.

Some people would say that I had – at that moment – merged with the source, or with God or the universal being. I have no idea. But it felt good. I've not tried to replicate the experience since – but I have had similar glimpses occasionally, usually when I'm driving.

As you develop The Watcher in you – your own CCTV camera – you get that slight sense that the thoughts are just happening, and that you don't have to get into them. Don't shout, 'Eh, big nose', just watch the colourful passing crowd of your mind with total impartiality.

> *Just watch the colourful passing crowd of your mind with total impartiality.*

CONSCIOUS BREATHING

Conscious breathing is very easy, yet very powerful. So for the increasingly lazy and carefree F**k It practitioner, there's not a lot to do or think about.

Breathing is a marvellous thing to play with. For most of us, breathing is something we don't (and don't have to) think about, ever. After the difficult, painful first few breaths when we're born, we tend to breathe pretty well for the rest of our lives.

Of course, if we have asthma or any other lung condition, we'll be very conscious of our breathing. But for many people, the only time they think about their breathing is if they feel sick and they're told to 'take some deep breaths (and put your head between your knees)' by their mothers.

Breathing is one of the miraculous automatic functions of our body: like the pumping of blood from our hearts, the exchange of oxygen and carbon dioxide, the regeneration of cells, the digesting of foodstuffs, the clearing of toxins, the balancing of acidity and alkalinity, and so on.

Our bodies just get on with their own business without us. And that's all very good. It would be a bummer to wake up in the morning and to have to go through a checklist of what to do:

* Breathing? Check.

* Heart pumping? Check.

* Correct hormones releasing? Check.

* Oxygen to carbon dioxide ratio 2:1? Check.

* pH level 8.5? Check.

* 20 per cent cells regenerating? Check.

* Engaging right side of brain? Check.

* Release adrenaline to begin worrying about the day? Check.

Now, here's the point. And it's a big one. Of all these numerous functions that are going on automatically all the time, breathing is the one that we can very easily play with and change.

Sure, if you really put your mind to it, you can slow your heart rate down. But it ain't that easy. Whereas now, sitting where you are, reading this, you can breathe more deeply, or more quickly, or you can hold your breath. And everything that you do consciously with your breath will have an effect on the rest of your body (and mind).

That's why Conscious Breathing is so cool.

If you sit and breathe consciously and deeply now for a few minutes, you will feel calmer, and a whole bunch of things will start to happen in your body:

* Your heart rate will slow down.

* You'll send more blood into your internal organs.

* You'll send more oxygen to your cells.

* You'll be releasing less adrenaline, thus relaxing the pressure on your overworked kidneys.

* You'll send a message to every cell that says, 'Hey, relax a little, it's not so bad after all.'

There are two sides to Conscious Breathing: bringing consciousness to how you are breathing now, and changing your breathing consciously.

Simply bringing consciousness to how you are breathing now allows you to get to know your breath. And it's a good idea to start doing this. Sure, as soon as you start to think about your breathing, it changes a little bit. It's hard to really catch it by surprise and see what it does when you're not looking. There's no dark wardrobe you can hide in and peek out of to see how you're breathing when you're not looking. Your lungs always know when you're in the wardrobe – no matter how small the crack is that you're looking out of.

But have a go. Notice what the breath feels like as it enters your nose (or mouth). Notice what moves when you're breathing. Are you breathing into your chest or belly? Are you breathing quickly or slowly? Are there any pauses in your breathing? Can you feel the effect of your breathing in other parts of your body? Concentrate very hard on your hands: is there anything going on in your hands as you breathe in and breathe out?

Notice how you breathe when you're relaxed. Notice how you breathe when you're in a big meeting at work, or when you're with your lover. Get to know your breathing: how it works, and how it changes. Start to learn your patterns and your ways of breathing. This is the first side of Conscious Breathing. The second side is to start playing with the breath – changing your breathing and breath patterns and seeing what happens with your body.

It's worth knowing a little bit about how our breathing works.

The inbreath is (obviously) when we take things in and expand. We take oxygen in. We take energy in. And our body expands with this. The chest or the belly expands, but so does the rest of the body, too. When you really get to know your breath and body, you'll feel the expansion in every part of your body: that's because every cell is expanding.

The outbreath is when we let things out and we relax. We let out carbon dioxide. We let out tension from our body. The whole body softens and relaxes and drops a little when we breathe out.

A little word on the 'energy' here. You might have lots of experience with energy, but you also might have no idea what I'm talking about. Energy – aka *chi*, or *qi*, or *prana*, or life-force, or life energy – is what they go on about a lot in the East, and what we have pretty much ignored here in the West. ·

First off, energy exists. It's not some esoteric idea. It exists and it is life. If we had no energy in our bodies, we'd be dead. Energy is a moving, tingling, magnetic-feeling force that moves through our bodies (and the body of anything else that's alive). Chinese medicine is all about the balancing of this energy to create a balanced physical system.

For now, if you know very little about this energy thing, simply be open to the possibility of feeling something new in your body. Or maybe starting to put a name to something you've already felt. The best time to spot this energy thing is when you are really relaxed. First, because – when you're really relaxed – energy flows. Second, because being relaxed will give you the space to feel the energy properly.

A little warning, though: beginning to feel your own energy can be seriously addictive. It feels gorgeous. It is like being bathed in light. It can feel ecstatic just to be sitting and feeling this life-force buzzing around your body. You can get hooked on this feeling and want to find ways to increase it. (But there are no side effects to this addiction; you will only feel better and get better.)

A little warning: beginning to feel your own energy can be seriously addictive.

And the best way to increase the feeling of chi, of course, is to say F**k It to everything, and breathe.

Conscious Breathing is the perfect aid for the F**k It practitioner.

Let's start with the F**k It Outbreath. If saying F**k It is about letting go of the things that matter and creating tension, then breathing out slowly is the best way to help this process. That's what the outbreath is: you release what you don't want; you let out all the waste gases and toxins and tensions that are not welcome in your body.

The quickest way to relax is to really slow down the outbreath. Really drag it out. And start to feel your body relaxing. You can exaggerate the effect of this even more if you add a sigh to the outbreath.

The sigh is an amazing tool in itself. You sigh when you're at the end of doing something difficult and strenuous. When you've finished work and poured yourself a whisky and you sit down on the sofa to watch an episode of your favourite soap, that's when you sigh. Sighing says to your body, 'That's it, you can relax and let go now.' Sighing is your way of saying, 'F**k It. No matter what's been going on today, now's my chance to sit back and relax.'

So if you want to trick your body into thinking that all the work's been done, and it can just sit back and relax, then SIGH.

Have a go at combining some F**k It thoughts with some sighing outbreaths. Choose whatever you want to say F**k It to at the moment; speak it out and then have a long, sighing outbreath. A quick warning here again: if you're reading this somewhere public, it may be best if you wait till later, when you're on your own. Or maybe just tone it down a bit… mumble your F**k It line, and then breathe out slowly. I'm sorry, I just don't want to get you into trouble.

I just don't want letters, you see. I don't want letters saying:

> *Dear Mr. Parkin,*
>
> *I was reading your book during a rather tedious recital of Brahms's Fifth Concerto at the local town hall, and I diligently carried out the F**k It breathing exercise. I said, 'F**k It to my husband's lingering gazes on Hilary Thrimble's ample breasts. F**k It.' I then breathed out with a long sigh, as you suggested. And to cut a long story short, I have been ostracized from Thricket Windon's polite social gatherings, which is a mortal wound for a woman of my standing…*

No, I don't want letters like that.

Just so you know, and in case it comes up, I'd like letters like this:

> *Dear Mr. Parkin,*
>
> *I read your words with a delight barely containable, and find all that you have to offer attracts me to the very core of my being. May I be so bold as to suggest a liaison next Wednesday evening at The Pimple and Shard? You can't miss me: I will be wearing a red rose pinned to one of the lapels covering my ample breasts.*
>
> *Yours,*
>
> *Hilary Thrimble*

Just so you know.

So, ahem, back to breathing. Where were we? Yes, The F**k It Outbreath.

Try it.

'I say F**k It to my bad back.' Then sigh and breathe out.

'I say F**k It to my bullying boss.' Then sigh and breathe out.

And so on.

Just say F**k It, then sigh and breathe out.

Whenever things matter too much. Whenever you feel tense or anxious or afraid. Just say F**k It, then sigh and breathe out. It works a treat.

But let's not forget the F**k It Inbreath. While the F**k It Outbreath is about letting go and relaxing, and saying no to things, the F**k It Inbreath is about pulling in energy and strength, and saying yes to things.

The F**k It Inbreath is about sucking in the energy to do what you want to do. And this is at least half the game in leading a F**k It life. If you want to get up from your desk and go and chat up the dishy new account director, take a deep breath, say F**k It and do it. If you want to go travelling, take a deep breath, say F**k It, hand in your notice and go book your flights. If you're tired of your boring relationship, take a deep breath, say F**k It and end it. Today.

In energy terms, the F**k It Outbreath is yin... relaxing, soft, letting go.

Whereas the F**k It Inbreath is yang... energetic, enthusiastic, embracing.

And if you know anything about Taoism, you'll know that you need a good balance of yang and yin to live harmoniously in this world.

The problem for most of us is that we live somewhere in between a good yanging and a good yinning life. So we don't go for things enough, we don't embrace life as vigorously as we could. And we don't relax and let go enough.

This is replicated in our breathing, just as everything in our lives is replicated in our breathing. If you look at anyone's outbreath and inbreath, they can look quite similar. The F**k It Inbreath is full of energy, though – try it, really fill up and pull in the energy. And the F**k It Outbreath is exactly the opposite. There should be no effort in letting the air out, just a letting go and relaxing.

The two breaths could not be more different. And each breath offers you the two sides of living the F**k It life.

Start practising breathing like this. Enjoy the active sucking in of energy that is the F**k It Inbreath. Then enjoy the absolutely passive letting-go that is the F**k It Outbreath. And you'll start to enjoy how this impacts on your life, too.

You'll give yourself the F**k It energy of the F**k It Inbreath to really go for it in life: to do what you really want to do, no matter what other people think.

And you'll give yourself the F**k It ability of the F**k It Outbreath to really not give a fuck about things that used to bother you and get you down.

So now let's look at how we can say F**k It to specific areas of our lives.

3

SAYING F**K IT

EVEN YOUR OWN MIND WILL RESIST YOUR IMPULSE TO SAY F**K IT

'Oh no it won't,' you say.

'Oh yes it will,' I say.

'Oh no it won't.'

'Oh yes it bloody well will.' Oh, I'm sorry, there are children present. Oh well, they shouldn't have come to a pantomime called *F**k It* anyway.

If your mind is anything like mine, it resembles a bad pantomime. And I have Piers Morgan playing Cinderella's Fairy Godmother in my head, which makes it all the more fascinating a place to be. Your head may be nothing like a pantomime, of course, but one thing I know for sure is that it will resist any impulse you have to say F**k It.

What the mind does

Knowing what your mind gets up to is a fun game. And it's a game that 'spiritual' people like to play. You see, once you know what's going on in there, you know what you're taking on, because the mind is often seen as the enemy.

We meditate (sometimes) in order to watch our thoughts and calm them down. We develop 'The Watcher' (maybe) in order to get some blessed detachment from the rabbiting of the mind. We become 'conscious' or 'aware' (if we're lucky) so that we're not simply controlled by what happens in the mind.

And remember, the 'mind' here is something more than the functioning brain. It's the thoughts we have; it's the feelings we have; and it's the receiving and processing of our senses: 'sensations'.

If you could watch your thoughts for just 30 minutes, you'd be amazed at what you saw (and heard).

I usually can't be arsed to do exercises, but if you have a mind that likes them, a good one to do is to write stuff down when you wake up. Just leave a pen and a notebook next to your bed, and once you've woken up (yes, you can have a pee if you want to, but you don't need to clean your teeth, not just yet, love), start writing.

Just write whatever comes into your head. No one is ever going to read it (if you don't want them to), and it's a good idea if *you* don't read it either, for a few days at least.

Just write whatever you are thinking. If you stop thinking, then stop writing. But when you think something again, just write it down. If what you are thinking is this: 'Ooh, I'm really hungry. I don't know what to have this morning… corn flakes or sugar puffs? Ooh, shall I invite the honey monster into my stomach… what do you think, honey monster? Tell 'em about the honey, mummy! Yes, honey, he said, but if it's honey, why do they call them sugar puffs? Should have called them honey puffs. Shit, I'm hungry. I wonder if I could stop writing and eat something? Shit, I'm tired, too – I must stop looking at porn into the night,' that's fine, just write it all down.

Do a week's worth and then have a little read through. You'll find that on the days you do it you'll tend to feel better than usual during the morning. This is because writing all that stuff down is a bit like having all the silly thoughts in your mind scraped out for a while.

If, like me, you can't be arsed to do this – and, unlike me, you can't even be bothered to have a play around with 'The Watcher' – the following is what the average mind sounds like. And this really is the average: I analyzed the minds of 100 people over the course of 100 days, and this is the average thought process of the average person.

Fleur is sitting in a coffee bar in London's Wardour Street. She's on her lunch break from her job as a marketing assistant in a publishing company. She is 31 years old, single and hungry.

> Oohh, what's this, then? Wafting in like she's the bloody queen. She's turned the corner, that's for sure. How does that happen? One day you're hot, the next day you're so not, and this lump is trying to cover her not-ness with racy rouge and that baggy boho outfit. Oh Christ, I might have known it: 'Chhiabbattaarrr with prooshhuttoo and motzerellllaa, please, or should I say perr favoray?' Christ, where does she think she is, Florence? You don't fool me, love: no matter how well you pronounce it, you're still having a lardy cheese and ham sandwich because you're past it and you don't care any more. Shit, I'm hungry. I'll nip into the health food shop and get some rice cakes. Even though everyone says they smell like farts. I can't see it – or, rather, smell it – myself.

I suppose if I could, I wouldn't eat them. So long live my rice-smelling rice cakes. My beloved rice cakes. Maybe a bit of honey on top, too. Oh shit, it's Andy. Please God, don't see me, don't see me. I haven't seen you, so don't see me. Christ almighty, he's talking to floppy tits. Stop the world, he's kissed her. What the fuck does he see in her? No Fleur, calm down, maybe he's her son? Shit, no, he's not. Oh Christ, oh Christ, got to get out, got to get out, got to get out. Phew, that's better. This calls for a fagerino; yes, a cigaretto is what this calls for. Shit, now I'm at it. Keep it together, keep it together. Just light it and you're away. Ahhhh.

This is what the mind does — well, the average mind, anyway. It rambles, it judges, it moans, it compares, it slags off, it analyzes, it resists, it rests in the negative, and it fears.

It matters to Fleur that she looks good; that she doesn't put on weight; that she doesn't look old; that she's attractive to men; that she stays 'hot'.

> **The mind has an addiction to the fears around the things that matter.**

The mind has a kind of addiction to the fears around the things that matter — an addiction to the negative. A lot of us moan and gossip about other people, and it creates a real pleasure in us. Even if people have harmed us, the moaning about it creates this subtle pleasure in us.

In the relentless comparison with, and judgement of, others, when people do anything that we don't approve of, it gives us pleasure because in some way we feel superior to them.

The possibility of saying F**k It to any of the things that really matter is, then, anathema to the mind. If you say F**k It and recognize that these things don't really matter, the mind has to give up its struggle, its resistance, its negativity, its judgement, and its constant moaning. And the mind is not going to give up these things easily. Even though they create misery in you, there is pleasure locked somewhere inside them: like a mint humbug, every hard and miserable emotion and feeling has a soft, delicious, chewy centre for the pain-obsessed mind.

SAY F**K IT TO FOOD

I read a figure recently about obesity in the USA. Apparently, 99 per cent of the population is obese. The only people (the 1 per cent) that aren't obese live in LA and are actors in films and on television. If you can't act, it means you're fat. Which of course creates problems at home:

'Chuck, have you bin eatin' donuts again?'

'No, Joline, I ain't been eatin' custard donuts with cinnamon bits, no, missy.'

Food is a problem in the developed world. (And, of course, lack of food is a bigger problem in the developing world, but…) If we're not battling with weight issues, we're struggling to eat the right things: with myriad intolerances and allergies, and with different advice coming from every direction.

In recent years, supermarkets have developed whole ranges of foods that don't seem to contain what you think they should, and this is what we've ended up eating:

* Wheat-free pasta
* Cocoa-free chocolate
* Caffeine-free coffee

* Sugar-free sweeteners

* Flour-free bread

* Dairy-free ice cream

* Sugar-free cakes

* Fat-free biscuits

* Meat-free sausages and burgers

It's just so funny. I'm looking forward to the following prefix: FOOD-FREE. I can't wait to try food-free lasagne, food-free pizza, food-free tiramisu. It'll go down a storm. Just as all the gluten-free and sugar-free stuff is for people who have been told they shouldn't eat these things but can't bear to go without the foods they were eating, so food-free lines will be designed for people who are fasting, or wanting to eat less, but need to go through the process of buying food from the supermarket, opening a packet and throwing things away.

Food-free lasagne is my favourite. It contains a microwavable container inside. You prick the plastic lid with a fork, then pop it in the microwave for just a minute. And it's done. You tear off the lid and inside are just the scraped remains of lasagne. You pop it straight in the bin. And you really feel as if you've gone through the whole meal experience.

That's the problem with fasting, you see. As well as being hungry enough to kill your fellow passengers on the Tube and eat them, you miss the whole thing around meals. So much spare time is created when you stop eating for a bit. And we don't know what to do with it. It's just time that you spend thinking about the food that you're not eating. So smear a plate with ketchup and do the washing up… you'll find your fast goes a whole lot better.

So why all the jokes? Because our stuff around food just consumes us. And I find this very funny. In one way or another we spend so long thinking about it. I'm a man and I think about food a lot. Maybe I'm a man who thinks like a woman. But from all that you hear, women are supposed to think about food a lot more than men.

And if we're thinking about sex every 10 seconds, I reckon we're thinking about food for at least seven of the other seconds. It's just amazing how any work gets done in this place.

And I'm being funny about it because that's the first step in the F**k It direction.

Our obsession with food is just crazy.

Our obsession with food is just crazy. And it is hilarious.

Food (like love and sex) is a major area of meaning for us. Though most of us are probably in denial about that. If we were asked to list the things that really matter to us, we probably wouldn't include food. But it's usually one of the things that matter most.

First, then, it's worth getting conscious around food. Start to notice how much you think about it. Notice what goes on when you think about food. Notice how you are when you're eating. Notice how you feel when you eat good food that you think you should be eating. And notice how you feel when you're eating bad food that you think you shouldn't be eating. Notice how you are when you see other people eating either extremely good food or extremely bad food. Notice how you feel when I keep asking you to notice how you feel. Anyway, just start to get an idea of how much food really matters to you.

Next, have a little inward giggle about how you are around food. Otherwise you'll cry.

Food matters so much to us for many reasons.

First, it is the great comforter. If you're uncomfortable about anything, then there's nothing more comforting than a bar of chocolate or a biscuit or some cake. And many of us nowadays spend a lot of time feeling uncomfortable but not wanting to face those feelings.

As well as giving you a surge of energy and feelings of happiness (the serotonin released when we eat chocolate, for example), food fills you up. We fill so we can't fill any more. We fill till we feel ill. We fill because the more we fill, the less we feel. And if we're feeling bad, then feeling is the last thing we want to do. We stuff ourselves until we go numb. There is – in many ways – no room for anything else.

Second, it has an effect on our health. Many conditions and diseases are caused by or heavily influenced by the foods we eat. With a modern diet, our bodies are too acidic and a breeding ground for illness. So it's no wonder that we try to eat this or that 'good' food, and try to cut out other foods. If you're ill and think your diet's got something to do with it, you could end up in the gluten-free, sugar-free, dairy-free, salt-free, meat-free and most certainly humour-free corner of the room.

Third, it has an effect on our body shape. Unlike the apparently positive and immediate effect of food as comforter, the negative effect of pounds being put on is a delayed one. You can stuff yourself silly for weeks and the effect on your body is relatively gradual. But the effect is certain. If you eat too much, you'll put on weight. And we live in fear of this. And when we do get overweight, we then live with the constant attempts to eat less. And in the battle with food, the time element always gets you: when you're pigging out, the pleasure is instant, but the pain is delayed. And when you're trying to eat less, the pain is instant, but the pleasure delayed.

Once you feel you understand more about what you're like about food, it's a good time to start mumbling F**k It a lot around food.

F**k It is about accepting things just as they are. So what would it feel like to start accepting how you are around food? The battle tends to be around eating the wrong things, or too much, and then feeling terrible about it. So when you next pig out, have a go at not beating yourself up about it. Say, 'F**k It, I always do this, no matter how hard I try, so I might as well accept this part of me.'

*F**k It is about accepting things just as they are.*

Even at the moment of choice. The moment when you're feeling down and you're going through the battle of whether to break your diet and the promises to yourself... just take the pressure off yourself. Say F**k It and either eat it and accept that or don't eat it and just get on with life. But don't make it such a big thing.

Stop making food such a big thing. If you've lost your job and your girlfriend's dumped you, then have a frickin' chocolate bar. In fact, get a cab down to the Mars factory in Slough and do the tour where you can scoop up fistfuls of Maltesers and stuff them into your mouth, or put away whole Mars Bars that haven't even had time to cool.

You'll feel better. And feeling better is good.

Say F**k It, and stop making food such a big thing.

Disease – as you probably know – is about dis-ease, being tense. The tension that you feel around eating the wrong or right foods is probably as much a contributor to your disease as anything that you put in your mouth.

I'd like to put on a white coat and do an experiment to demonstrate this. I've got two people in my lab with exactly the same health condition. A disease that they believe is affected by food. I've placed them under a trance and am about to give them some food.

The first person, let's call him First for the sake of anonymity, is given a chocolate éclair (you may not remember these, they may be left in the 1970s, but they're basically hot dogs but made with pastry, chocolate and cream). First is told (under trance, remember) that this food is going to do him the world of good and will make him feel much better immediately; it may even lead to a healing of his condition.

The second person, let's call him B for the sake of confusion, is given a wholefood salad with nuts and seeds. And he's told that he can't resist this food because it's so delicious but it will undoubtedly have a negative effect on his condition.

First and B are plugged into lots of machines with dials and things that beep, and as they eat the food we start to monitor them.

First is completely relaxed but is eating something that should immediately affect his condition. But there is absolutely no beeping or swinging of dials on the machines.

B is very tense but is making 'mmmm' noises as he eats his salad. After just one mouthful, things beep and dials swing and his condition immediately deteriorates.

We monitor First and B for 6 hours after the consumption of the food, and the pattern is the same:

* First's consumption of the chocolate éclair has no effect on his condition. The state of his mind has completely cancelled out the anticipated physical reactions.

* B's consumption of the health-giving nutty salad has caused him to become ill.

You see? This is science. I'm wearing a white coat and things have been beeping, so it must be true.

But it's worth thinking about when you're trying to resist some bread and putting yourself through agony because you're scared it will aggravate your slightly extended bowel condition.

Body shape, the biggie. So much has been written about diets and the effect of diets, it's hardly true. People consume diets as voraciously as they consume the food the diet books are telling them not to eat.

Well, it's time to Fuck the diet.

It's time to Fuck the diet.

All diet books are useless, and they're laying the world's forests to waste. So pop all your diet books in the recycling bin and plant a tree. In fact, plant a fruit tree, then eat the fruit. You'll lose weight and do the world a favour.

Just as with health, it's the tension around it all that's causing the problem.

So, first of all, accept things as they are: maybe you're a little chubby, maybe you're a complete porker, but accept yourself as you are. At least for a few minutes… then go back to the self-loathing until you can build up the accepting bit to more minutes. But have a go.

Accept your eating habits as they are. You know that, for you, eating is just a merry-go-round. It seems you have no control in the end. And after a patch of eating less, you lose it and eat a whole shelf-full of biscuits (and we're talking the shelf of a supermarket, not a shelf in your kitchen cupboard).

It's also worth accepting that – to one degree or another, and like every other human being walking this Earth – you're fucked up. You have emotional problems, anxieties, neuroses, fears, low self-confidence…

Whatever it is, you ain't too happy with yourself and life, and you're eating to feel better.

Most of us do it. Most of us won't admit it. But look at that word – most – you're not alone in this. So you're fucked up… yes, you're human.

All this acceptance will have the definite effect of relaxing you.

Say F**k It to your diet. And F**k It when the voices start coming up. How about saying F**k It and eating what you really fancy for your next meal? Say F**k It afterwards when you start to feel bad. And go with it and see what happens. If you put on a bit of weight, say F**k It.

My bet is that you will start to get over your issues around food.

My bet is that once you can eat what the hell you want, you won't need to stuff the whole of a birthday cake into your mouth in one go because you know you can have more later or tomorrow if you want.

My bet is that without so much tension around 'good' and 'bad' foods, you may well start to want to eat some of the foods that you thought were 'good' but were so painful to eat. You'll find that you actually like eating these foods. But don't start thinking they're 'good'; just eat what you want and see what happens.

And my bet is that, eventually, you will start to lose weight. If you're still saying F**k It, you shouldn't really care too much. If it matters less to you that you're putting on weight, then it should matter less to you that you're losing it. Sure, treat yourself to a little smile as you see the scales beneath your feet… but you can still say F**k It and have a choccie bar to celebrate.

So Fuck your diet and start saying F**k It. Accept how things are, and how you are, because everything is OK as it is – let food and your body shape matter less to you. And observe what all these zen dudes have been monking on about for so long: that when you lose your desire for something, that's the moment when you start to get it.

SAY F**K IT IN YOUR RELATIONSHIPS

And thus we enter the minefield. This is maybe the most difficult area of your life to understand how saying F**k It in any way can do anything but fuck up your relationships. Let's see why.

Relationships are like the Piccadilly Circus of your meaning city.

They are indeed. Relationships are where it all happens, where all the action is, where a lot of your attention is focused and where collisions often occur. The other areas of your meaning city are more predictable: your job is more predictable, as are your friends (generally), as is your health, etc., etc.

Relationships are like the Piccadilly Circus of your meaning city.

But with relationships, what matters *really* matters. The meaning of it all affects us to our very core. A relationship is about us... and the most intimate way we deal with the outside world. The stakes are higher. And everything is invested:

* If something hurtful is said, we feel it deeply.

* If we don't feel heard, we feel like children.

* If we think we love them more than they do us, we feel pain.

* If we think they love us more than we love them, we feel guilt.

* If we get excitement from someone outside the relationship, we feel confused.

* If they get excitement from outside the relationship, we feel
  jealous.

If life as we live it is about the relationship between us and the
outside world, then your relationship with a partner is the finest
thread of that relationship.

In a relationship, we are deeply attached to success, and immensely
pained by failure. Because everything in a relationship matters so
much, the potential for pain is enormous. And many of us do live
out the fairly constant pain of our relationship(s). This means that
the early days/weeks/months of relationships can often be the most
turbulent, as things matter so darn much.

After years within a relationship, things tend to matter less, the stakes
are lower and the potential for pain reduces.

In relationships, your meaning environment can change rapidly. This is
commonly known as falling in love. When you fall in love, other things
matter less. Sometimes the only thing that matters is that person. All
your normal perceptions of the world go out of the window. Any
rationality that you apply to your life can evaporate.

So people who fall in love commonly do the following: leave families
they previously adored, give up jobs and positions, lose friends, change
their beliefs, lose their dress sense, lose *any* sense, start listening to
music they previously thought was naff.

Love does funny things to people. Zillions of songs have been
written about just this effect. Romantic love, then, is apparently a key
challenge to the F**k It way of living, as love seems often to be about
the meaning of someone else to you and the subsequent attachment
and dependency. We think that these qualities are part and parcel of
loving someone.

Saying F**k It can have some surprising effects. The problem is that it's very hard to see what F**k It can do in a relationship. How could any good possibly come of your partner feeling less attached to you or feeling less like you're the centre of their world? We love all that dependency and attachment stuff in relationships.

> *Saying F**k It can have some surprising effects.*

Have you ever played the reductionist love game with anyone? It goes something like this:

'Would you still love me if I was really fat?' 'Yes, of course.'

'Would you still love me if I'd been scarred in an accident?' 'Yes, of course.'

'Would you still love me if I had no legs?' 'Yes, of course.'

'Would you still love me if I had no arms?' 'Yes, of course.'

'Would you still love me if I couldn't see?' 'Yes, of course.'

'Would you still love me if I couldn't hear?' 'Yes, of course.'

'Would you still love me if I had no teeth?' 'Yes, of course.'

'Would you still love me if I couldn't think? If I was in hospital in a vegetative state?' 'Err, yes, of course.'

'Would you still love me if I was dead?' 'Yes, of course, darling.'

'What, forever?' 'Yes, for you, forever, darling.'

It's a very funny game. And a very moving game, too. It's one that works out well if you keep on saying 'yes'. But what is it that the person is asking? Would you still love me if I was reduced down to the very point of non-existence… would you still love me then?

Phew, that's some pressure: 'Yes, even if you weren't there at all, in any sense, I would still love you.'

In love we want a lot. We want all the attention. We want it to last forever. We want it to be perfect. And we throw everything we have into these desires.

This is attachment and dependency. And this is a very obvious and large potential for pain.

The possibility of saying F**k It is like the story of the two-dimensional people.

Imagine people living in a two-dimensional world: nothing has a three-dimensional shape, everything is lines and shading. These people simply cannot conceive of a three-dimensional world – it is beyond their understanding. If you tried to explain it to them they wouldn't get it. But take them into this new world. Let them live in it for a while. And they instantly get it and see how utterly amazing it is compared to their old 2D world.

This is what it's like to start saying F**k It to things. And especially in relationships. From your position in a loving attachment to someone, it's very difficult to see how feeling less attachment towards them could improve things. But let's have a go.

Think of a relationship where you were deeply in love with someone: smitten by them (and this may well be your present relationship, of course). Remember what it felt like to be attached to them: loving their attention and looks… waiting for their calls… cherishing time with them above everything else. And remember the flip side, too: getting anxious, wondering whether they loved you as much as you loved them… getting jealous easily… getting frustrated with yourself for being so dependent on someone.

Now imagine what it would have been like to have taken things a little less seriously. Imagine if you'd not taken things so personally. Imagine if you hadn't worried about whether it would last forever. Imagine hanging on less to the relationship and letting the other person breathe. Imagine them mattering a tad less to you. Imagine that 'you' weren't at stake in the relationship.

And here's the strange thing: it doesn't mean that you love this person any less. In fact, this may be where definitions of love start to strain at the leash. Because the clingy, attaching romantic love that we and everything in our society supports as 'love' can transform into another kind of 'love' when we stop clinging.

It's an unexpected outcome, but when there is less meaning, the love seems to increase. Try it, but it's a 3D world for normally 2D people.

Part of the reason for this, of course, is due to tension and relaxation. When you are attached and dependent, there is an enormous tension in the relationship. There is no room for anything to move. As soon as something shifts, things start to snap, like a very tight spring just snapping.

When you relax everything – when you relax out of your attachment and investment in the relationship – there is more space and room. And just as *chi* flows more readily in a relaxed body, the love flows more readily in a relaxed relationship.

Love flows more readily in a relaxed relationship.

So if you're scared of your man/woman running off with someone else, say F**k It – there's plenty of men/women for you out there.

Whatever the issues and tightness in your relationship, see what it's like to say F**k It to them. Just speak out your issue now. Then say

79

F**k It and see how it feels.

'I don't feel she finds me attractive like she used to… Well, F**k It.'

And so on.

Whatever stage your relationship is in, poke your head out for a mo and see what it's like when you feel that things don't quite matter as much. Feel the relaxation. Feel the freedom. Then carry on with your life and see what happens.

Like the energy that flows through a newly relaxed body, love and energy might start to flow more through you and your relationship. Well, this is what could happen:

* A new life enters your existing relationship and you move to a different level

* You realize that this relationship is wrong for you and you leave it

* The love grows in your relationship, and at the same time you recognize you want love from other people, too.

The third one is potentially the most confusing. You might find that the increased love you're feeling is hard to contain (in your relationship). And you might work towards a more 'open' relationship. This is also commonly known as 'having your cake and eating it'. It recognizes the perpetual and opposite urges that most human beings have: to be with one person forever… and to be with everyone else, too (usually for a considerably shorter time, such as one night).

This appears to be a difficult and dangerous path. But are monogamous relationships easy and safe?

If the whole idea freaks you out, say F**k It and move on. One day you might want to, err, F**k It, and you can come back then and re-read this bit.

SAY F**K IT TO ILLNESS AND DISEASE

A lot of people are forced into the world of alternative therapy – and the accompanying spiritual aspects – through a desire to cure illness and disease. Either conventional medicine has failed them and they're casting their net more widely for a cure, or they don't trust conventional medicine from the start.

And alternative medicine has a lot to offer. It seems that – from the bewildering array of therapies on offer – one will provide a cure for you. The problem is, though, that what's on offer is so bewildering. It's tempting – if you suffer from any kind of illness – to work your way through the list until you find the one that magically does it for you.

In this respect, the difference between conventional and complementary medicine is fascinating.

It's ironic that the approach with complementary medicine is holistic, but the response is compartmentalized. So most therapists will treat you as a whole: mind, body and spirit are all linked, and all physical symptoms are just one indicator of an overall imbalance. But the response is then compartmentalized: there will be perhaps 50 different complementary ways of dealing with your overall imbalance.

Whereas with conventional medicine, the approach is compart-mentalized, but the response is uniform. So most doctors will treat the part of you that is sick, often ignoring other factors of your 'whole' being. If you have a problem with your eyes, you're sent to the eye specialist. But the response is then uniform. The problem with your eyes is likely to be treated in the same way by any eye specialist around the world.

So complementary medicine is like a backwards version of conventional medicine.

If you are – or have been – ill, chronically or acutely, or even mildly, I suspect you've tried your fair share of alternative therapies. So you recognize the challenge of facing this immense list of possibilities. Where do you start? What's best for you?

Here in Italy, the complementary medicine world has taken another path. And it's a good deal simpler. The conventional medicine blueprint simply has a holistic mirror image in the form of homoeopathy. There are, of course, many other therapies sitting in the wings, but for most people the choice is simple: they go conventional or they go natural and homoeopathic. A homoeopathic consultation is just like going to your doctor (except the medicines are more expensive); in fact, there's a good chance s/he is a conventional doctor as well. Many pharmacies – even in the smallest villages – offer homoeopathic remedies, too.

So it's become a welcome and easy alternative for people disillusioned with conventional medicine.

You'll recognize the desperation to find a cure.

If you are – or have been – ill, you'll also recognize the desperation to find a cure. And I think those who are interested in the world of alternative therapy feel this even more deeply.

This works on several levels. First, very obviously, if your condition is causing you pain, discomfort, embarrassment, then you're desperate to sort it out. If you can't sleep or you feel tired all the time, or it hurts to pee, or your skin is irritated, or your belly distended, or your scalp flakey, or your hands shaky… you really want to get rid of those symptoms.

And you'll go to just about any lengths to sort it out: you'll eat a ridiculously strict diet; you'll do calming breathing exercises for an hour a day; you'll boil up foul-smelling herbs; you'll let someone place 10 fine needles in sensitive parts of your body; you'll try to do yoga positions that mean you have to hook your heel over your ear; you'll take expensive medicines that contain no 'medicine'.

And, you know, I think it's understandable – laudable even. I've been there myself, and have all the badges.

Second, there is something inherent in the holistic world that perpetually drags us towards the goal of 'wellness'. If health is wholeness, then sickness is not. If we are not completely well and bouncing with aliveness, then we are somehow not whole. And this is a tremendous burden to carry, as many of us are not well all (or even much) of the time. Yes, I know, symptoms and illnesses are seen as cleansing and purifying for the body… *the body is naturally moving itself towards wellness, and illness can therefore be seen as 'good'*. But it's the same thing in the end: illness is good only because it's momentarily perceived as a means to an end, which is wellness. It's good only because of what it's leading to.

In the world of holistic medicine, there is an attachment to wholeness and wellness: an aim for completeness that mirrors the spiritual path of, say, a yogi who aims for spiritual 'union'.

And that's how it is.

But you know what? It's tiring and it's boring. Just like any attachment to anything is eventually tiring and boring. It's tiring and boring to wander from one therapy to another, achieving different levels of success. If one therapy seems to be working, you really go for it and get your hopes up. Then it seems to stop working and you get depressed. Every therapy is offered evangelically by someone who was 'cured' by it, and they think it will do the same for you. But while it may help, it's usually not the cure.

Of course, there's the chance that it may be. Those hot stones under your eyelids may well cure you of your curly toenail syndrome.

But I'd prefer to look at another possibility.

Some people get so tired and bored with trying everything, and spending lots of money, and investing so much energy, that they simply give up. They say one big F**k It, and finally give up wanting to be whole and well and perfect. They're still feeling the pain and discomfort, but they just say F**k It and give in to it. Nothing makes any difference anyway, so why should they go through the added pain of hoping it's going to go away?

They give in fully to their condition. They surrender completely to their pain. They give up wanting to be any different from how they are, just as they are, now. They probably start eating things they haven't eaten for a while, they may start drinking again. What they certainly do is RELAX. The one thing you'll always do when you really say F**k It is relax.

Say Fk It and surrender completely to your pain.**

And you know what happens? Perhaps not straight away; perhaps not for a little while. But they tend to get better. This takes them by surprise, because they'd given up needing it. But they get fully better and achieve what they'd always wanted. Only they're genuinely not bothered about their health any longer, so it doesn't matter that much – even though they're suddenly in full health.

I'm describing a natural process here: the natural way to say F**k It. But if you're reading these words there's a good chance you're tired and bored and ready to give up, too. Don't say F**k It to cheat the gods, secretly really caring about your health and thinking that it's a darn clever way to get well. But the moment you stop caring so much about your health is the moment things will start to shift.

> ## Don't say F**k It to cheat the gods.

When you care less – or maybe not at all – it doesn't mean you necessarily stop eating well or exercising or meditating, or even having acupuncture, but the desperation and investment in doing these things disappear.

I now eat well because I really like the taste of fresh vegetables and fruit. I also like the taste of ice cream, though, so I eat that, too.

I now exercise because I really love the feeling of screaming down a hill on a mountain bike, and the sense of physical tiredness in my body… not because it will (one day) contribute to my reaching full, whole health.

I now meditate for the energy that spreads through my body when I do so, but to me, it feels no different from the energy that spreads through my body when I get angry.

What happens, then? As usual, it's all down to relaxation. I – like many people – recognized the power of relaxation to cure illness a long time ago. I trained in Tai Chi and Chi Kung to use movement, breathing and chi to totally relax my body. I trained in hypnotherapy to use the mind to totally relax myself. I've tried just about every method of relaxation that's available. Because I knew a long time ago something that a lot of people don't realize: problems have trouble existing in the face of total relaxation. Physical, mental, emotional and spiritual problems have little to stick to in the face of total relaxation.

I knew this. I practised the methods to a high level. And yet very little changed. Why? Because I still had aims, attachments and myriad meanings. And these are all basically tension. The bummer is this: if you want health and you use even the best relaxation method to try to get it, your very wanting of that health is a tension that the method is unlikely to be able to break down.

> **Give up wanting anything, and everything will come.**

So the most advanced relaxation method you'll ever find is not caring and not wanting… saying F**k It.

Give up wanting anything, and everything will come. (But of course you can't want that!)

SAY F**K IT TO MONEY

In our world of meaning, money means a lot. This is, of course, not true for everyone, but generally:

* If we don't have much, we wish we had some and that all our money worries would go away

* If we have a moderate amount of money, enough not to worry about bills and paying for holidays, we dream of having more, being able to drive a better car or live in a bigger house

* If we are wealthy, we still tend to want more, to be financially independent, or to have a holiday home in a foreign land

* If we are stinking rich, we tend to worry that we could lose everything in the next crash.

If we're not rich, we tend to resent those who are. We judge those who flash money around; we think that 'money can't make you happy'; we know that 'they can't take it with them', and we think it's 'indecent'.

If we're rich, we can be quite defensive about our money: it may be important to us that we 'worked hard for it', or that we're not really *that* rich (not compared to really rich people), and we might deliberately not 'flash it around' by buying a moderate car and not a flashy one.

So, whether you're broke or loaded, money brings its issues. You probably have your issues and judgements around money. You may think that it's OK to be 'comfortably off' but that having too much is immoral.

Well, F**k It. How about having no judgement around money, and accepting things just as they are?

Money is just an abstract means of exchange, after all. It's the messenger boy in the exchange deal between you and the world. And you know what they say about the messenger: don't kill him.

> *Have no judgement around money, and just accept things as they are.*

This is simply about exchange. If what you have to offer is worth enough to other people, then they'll give you lots of things in return. So, for a moment, imagine that there wasn't any money. If enough of you read this book, you'll all offer me something for it. I'm in particular need of flowers for the garden at the moment. So you all give me some flowers. The more of you who read this, the more flowers I'll receive.

By next summer, my garden should be full of flowers and looking beautiful. And that's all being rich is. I offer something you like, and you give me something in return for it. I'm happy that I've given you something of value. And I'm happy that my previously barren garden is now full of flowers. That's beautiful: there's nothing dirty or immoral about that, is there?

See the same for what you do. When you work (or whatever you normally do for money), imagine that you're simply offering something of value to the world, and the world values this and gives you something for it. The world values what you do by paying your bills, buying your clothes, taking you out for dinner, sending you on holiday and turning up at your house with a new car.

You are simply in a constant process of exchange for value with the world. The more the world values what you do and what you are giving, the more it will give back.

What tends to happen is that the more you value yourself, the more the rest of the world will tend to agree and value you as well. So start by valuing yourself. Listen to the corporate guru L'Oréal: Because You're Worth It.

The more you value yourself, the more the world will value you.

Enjoy the process of exchange: whether big or small. If you're happy to be humble and self-contained, enjoy the small things that the world brings you for the things that you offer.

If you want to go out and really offer something amazing to the world, lap up the attention, and value what you're given in return. Don't be resentful of those who are being given a lot for what they're offering to the world. Enjoy it: enjoy that the world is generous enough to give to those it values.

And don't put any limits on what you think the world should give you. If people continue to read this book, and keep on giving me flowers, I will continue to accept those flowers and fill my garden with them. One problem I might run into is not having enough water to keep them all alive. So at some point I'll have to stipulate that, while I'd still love to receive flowers, I'd prefer ones that don't need much water. Yes, I could set up a special cactus garden.

And when that is full, I'll truly know I'm officially Stinking Rich.

Say F**k It to some of your money issues, then, by picturing money as simply your exchange relationship with the world. But also say F**k It to money full stop. Money doesn't matter that much, really. A lot of our tension around money is the fear of having none.

So it's a good idea to imagine what it would be like to have none, so you can face that fear head-on. Imagine losing all the money and possessions that you have. What would you do? In a society like ours I would have thought that most of you could imagine how you would be able to cope. You may have to go on benefits while you look for a job. But then you find a job of some sort, and you find enough money to rent your own flat… etc., etc.… and you're off.

If you lost everything, you wouldn't die.

So lose your fear of losing your money. The world will still value what you have to offer, and it will lavish you with gifts once more.

Lose your fear of losing your money.

Any attachment around money is, of course, tension. Attachment to getting more, or attachment to keeping what you have – it's all tension.

Saying F**k It to money releases that tension and leaves just softness and relaxation. And, as we're seeing in other areas, when there's relaxation, things flow. It's the same with the value exchange we call money. When we relax our hold on money, things tend to flow more naturally. That means that things tend to flow naturally in both directions. If you stop being so uptight about losing money, then you may well start to spend more, invest more and be more generous. And this gets the flow going. You'll tend to find that more money then starts to come your way.

I like this theory of money — keeping money in circulation. I do, however, regret sharing the idea with my wife, Gaia. She often returns home with bags of clothes, saying, 'I'm just keeping the money circulating.' I shake my head, raise my eyebrows and say, 'Oh F**k It.'

Money. If you have none, say F**k It and enjoy life as it is. If you have some, say F**k It and start enjoying people valuing you. If you have oodles, say F**k It and start basking in the fruits of the world thinking you're such an amazing person that it throws so much at you.

SAY F**K IT TO FAME

Gaia very nearly persuaded me not to write this section: she wondered how relevant it would be to most people. But then we met the guests who'd just arrived for the latest F**k It Retreat, and there were two famous people among them. Boom. They were lovely, and we talked a lot about the fame and success thing. And no, I'm not going to tell you who they were.

This process of debating something (should I write a section on fame), then a big coincidence happening (two famous people turning up) is, in itself, a beautiful example of free F**k It living.

When you begin to live more freely, and open up, and fix things less, some wonderful things happen. All you have to do is open your eyes a little more. It's all there to be seen when you look. Sometimes, it feels to me as if life is like a play put on just for my benefit. In a play, we know that everything has significance: every word and every action is part of the whole scheme, and therefore has meaning. In a play (a good one, at least), nothing is superfluous. Every single action actually means something.

When you begin to live more freely, wonderful things happen.

It's tempting to think that real life is the opposite of this: that everything is random, unrelated and meaningless. Whereas when you look harder (but with a soft vision), you see all the links, the beautiful hidden meanings, and the apparent coincidences that are nothing of the sort. The world's shamanic cultures referred to this as the 'web of life', and they saw 'Great Spirit' as part of everything – speaking to them through every phenomenon, through every event and action.

So, I'm going to talk about fame, and how to be free in this glittery Fame Town. And I'm not just talking about big-fame fame. This is not just about LA fame. There are huge numbers of people who enjoy fame in their own areas. If someone does exceptionally well in their particular field, they'll probably enjoy a degree of fame in that field.

But even at a larger fame level, there are many more 'famous' people than there used to be, thanks to an explosion of media channels, and our consumption of them. And we've gobbled it all up. Fame has become a game in itself – a huge market where 'ordinary' people bid in a variety of ways to become famous. In so doing they become semi-famous, or, if they're lucky, they become full-fat famous.

Fame has become an aim in itself, too. When I was growing up, we wanted to be something: a footballer or a rock star or a management consultant. We knew that fulfilling our dream would maybe lead to fame and fortune, but we didn't want to achieve it *because* of that: we wanted to play football for a living, or perform on a stage in front of thousands of people, or enjoy the raw thrill of instituting a change management programme in a large quoted company.

And that, to me, seems to be the answer in Fame Town. Whether you want to become one of the famous, or you're already famous in your own area, or you're Brangelina, do what you love, keep doing what you love, do it for the love of it, and don't get carried away by the fame thing. That's saying F**k It to Fame: that the fame doesn't matter so much and you're just doing what you love.

> *Do what you love, and don't get carried away by the fame thing.*

Sure, fame can be lovely. It's wonderful for your self-esteem if everyone thinks you're great. But if everyone thinking you're great is the sole source of your self-esteem, you're in for a rocky ride, as the world of fame invariably has its ups and downs.

SAY F**K IT TO THE WEATHER

I giggle when people complain about the weather.

Every day we are surrounded by things that don't suit us. The sound of the dog barking next door, the way our partner ignores us over breakfast, the traffic jam on the way to work, being handed another project with a tight deadline, being hassled by the office bore…

And we believe that we can exert some control over these things that get us down: we could shoot the dog, tell our partner to give us some attention, leave for work earlier, say no to the project and tell the office bore to go bore someone else.

A very harmonious way to live with an awkward world would be to try to change what pisses us off, or just accept it as it is.

The difficult way to live is to not do a thing about what pisses us off, and not accept it either… so we spend our days being pissed off about things we're not willing to do anything about. And this is how many of us live.

If this sounds somewhat dysfunctional, then, to me, it seems hilariously dysfunctional to start complaining about the weather. Because this really is one thing we can do nothing about. Usually not today, anyway. In the long term, you can move abroad and buy yourself some different weather, but for now, this is it.

To complain about the weather is the most absurd example of not accepting the world as it is.

So say F**k It to the weather, whatever it is, especially in a country like the UK. Relax into the weather. Look up at the grey skies and think that it's a little like living in a Tupperware container. Enjoy the sound of rain on the car roof. Huddle close to the fire in your local pub when it's cold. And soak up the sun whenever it comes out.

SAY F**K IT TO BEING A PEACEFUL PERSON

For a long time I wanted to be a peaceful and calm person. I remember writing, 10 years ago, a list of the things I wanted the most. Top of the list was Peace (just in case you're wondering, next up was an original Chopper bike).

I spent years in my search for peace: practising Chi Kung and meditation every day, trying to work through the issues that made me un-peaceful, getting to know people who seemed to live in peace. I found a good deal of peace through practice, especially Chi Kung. And I imagined that if I could just practise more I would eventually end up perpetually in the Chi Kung state (this is a light trance state where you are completely relaxed and *chi* is flowing evenly round your body).

I imagined myself as a cool mountain: light activity on the surface, but rock-solid deep down.

I imagined myself as a Taoist monk: gently and calmly carrying out the day's activities in peace and mindfulness. I imagined myself as being like my friend Richard, who remains calm and peaceful no matter what is happening.

I imagined that if only I worked harder at being peaceful, I would eventually make it.

But no matter how hard I tried, no matter how much I practised and how much I looked at my issues, I kept coming up against one big problem on my path to peace: me. Even if I meditated for three hours, I would still return to me in the end.

And this is me: sure, I can be peaceful and calm, generous and kind, centred and balanced. But I can also be stressed and anxious, angry and aggressive, afraid and nervous, selfish and cold.

I recognized, therapeutically, that it was important to let out the 'negative' emotions. And I imagined that if I looked at them enough, and vented them enough (in a healthy environment, of course), they would eventually be vented, and be no more.

Then one day I realized that what I was doing was not that different from what my mother has always done, and I have so heavily judged: as a Christian, she regards her 'good' side as holy and of God, and her 'bad' side as sinful, and sin is of the Devil. I've always had trouble understanding how anyone can look at themselves and their own characteristics and believe that they come from a dark and evil force. When she eats too much, she regards it as gluttony, a sin.

For most of us it's a bummer, but for her, it's a sin. So she spends her life trying to battle the dark force with her God-inspired light sabre of peace. But the Darth Vader of sin is always there for her, often in the form of oven-baked chicken nuggets or Black Forest gateau.

In response to these perpetual episodes of Christian *Star Wars*, I celebrated the power of the whole human being. I loved being me, in whatever form that took, from an early age.

But then somehow I got into a peace trip. And, yes, one day I realized that wanting to be peaceful and monk-like was just making me judgemental about all the bits in me that aren't. In my own way I was making relaxation, peacefulness and generosity right and holy. And I was making stress, anger and selfishness wrong and unholy.

So I said F**k It to trying to be anything other than who I am, in this moment. I stopped judging myself. And shit, what a relief that was. What a relief it *is*.

> *I said F**k It to trying to be anything other than who I am.*

Every emotion I feel is absolutely OK, just as it is. If I feel love and peace, that is just the same as when I feel fear and anxiety. This is what 'acceptance' and 'non-judgement' really mean. You can't say: 'OK, I won't get so down about my anger, but of course it's better to be peaceful.' No. They are both the same. That is non-judgement.

And there's a fantastic side effect to accepting yourself for whoever you are: you start accepting other people for who they are, too. It may not happen straight away, but it definitely starts to happen. And it happens for a very simple reason: whenever you judge other people, it simply comes from a non-acceptance of yourself in all your parts.

Jesus himself started to hint at this when he said: 'Love one another as you love yourself.' Now, I know he hadn't had the privilege of training in Gestalt psychoanalytical theory back then, but he did miss out one darn big thing in this: that most people don't love themselves at all. And it's because they don't love themselves that they're so shitty to everyone else.

Sorry, Jesus, but may I suggest that this would have been a better line: 'Love yourselves, dudes, then you'll start loving everyone else, and we can all get together in one big, hippie, free-love festival type thing and strip off our sandals and rub each other's beards. Peace and love, dudes.'

Maybe Jesus actually did say this, but stuffy old Matthew, Mark, Luke and John took the good bits out. Judas was probably sitting there smoking a reefer saying, 'Hey, dudes, what about the bit He said about the love fest? That was far out.'

And Matthew just turned round and punched him.

Judas protested: 'Shit, man, it was only a thought.'

And Luke stood up and kicked him hard in the balls.

Judas shut up after that.

Perhaps you too want to be a calm and peaceful person. Perhaps you want to be a kind and generous person. Or perhaps you want to be a ruthless and cold person. Whenever you define the limits of what you want to be, you're going to make the other parts of yourself 'wrong', and that means you're on a hiding to nothing. Even the person who wants to be ruthless and cold is going to feel love and warmth occasionally, and he'll start kicking himself for having those feelings.

So say F**k It to whatever you want to be. And just be who you are. There is no need to be anything else. There is no need to self-develop, or improve. There is no need to be like anyone else.

*Say F**k It to whatever you want to be, and just be who you are.*

You are just fine exactly as you are right now. Just feel that now. All those bits of you that you don't like, that you're embarrassed about, they're all fine. What you think of as your worst side is just the same as what you think of as your best side.

When you are angry, anxious, jealous, ruthless, that's all the same as when you're calm, peaceful, generous and loving.

Because that is you. And it's me. And everyone else on this planet. And to pretend otherwise would mean we'd have to go off and start a religion with the catchy title: 'I am only this and not that, you know. Really.'

That's all religions are, really. Only they add another line, which always gets me down, so that in total it becomes: 'I am only this and not that, you know. Really. And if you are what I think I'm not, then you're wrong. And you'll burn in hell for it.'

What we're talking about is being 'holistic' in the true sense. As a whole person we are many things. In fact, as a whole person we are everything. As a whole person I feel every emotion that has ever been felt by anyone. And I sometimes feel them all in one day. I can even feel them all when I'm watching a good episode of *Coronation Street*.

SAY F**K IT TO PARENTING

If you don't have children, then it may be worth skipping this section, as I will be talking directly to parents. And you may get a bit bored. Just like you do whenever any of your friends have kids and all they can talk about are nappies, vaccinations, which schools to book the baby into and how cute their little one looks when he's having a shit. Quit now and turn to the next bit, please. I can't bear to put you through it.

And that's parenting for you in a nutshell. Those who don't have kids can't understand what it's like, can they? It's impossible for us parents to understand before we have children what it's going to be like.

I can see the whole process was designed to ease you into the idea of having children around. After all, you get nine months – nine whole months, that's practically a year of your life – to start getting used to the idea. And there are lots of aspects of pregnancy that allow you to start to get the idea of parenthood: the woman is being sick all the time so you get used to the smell; she starts to snore, so you get used to disturbed nights; she can't do anything risky, so you get used to staying at home and watching television rather than clubbing and taking drugs; she gets so big that you get used to having less room in bed.

But nothing – not even these nine months – can prepare you for what it's like to have children. We have non-identical twin boys, Arco and Leone, who are now 12. At 4 a.m. on the night after they were born, I got up for the hundredth time to change one of them – which was a weird experience in itself because no one had ever told me they wouldn't be shitting; well, shit, for a while they'd be shitting melted chocolate. So there I was in the anaemic early morning light, getting accustomed to a new routine of wiping shit from my baby's body and re-applying the plastic safety net ready for the next expulsion.

And I looked around and thought, 'No, this is OK. I can do this. Yes, I feel tired. But I can do it. I can get through it.'

But then I realized that I didn't have to get through just this one night. That it wasn't like working through the night on a last-minute college essay, handing it in just before the 10 a.m. deadline and then going to sleep for a few days. No, siree. This certainly wasn't just tonight. This was tonight and tomorrow night and the night after and the night after that and on and on and on.

And I groaned.

But then one of my new baby boys chuckled. And I melted.

And over the following few weeks I learned that everything is designed to be in perfect balance. The utter hell of the first few weeks, mainly caused by severe sleep deprivation, was perfectly balanced by the absolute heaven of having two such incredible beings suddenly appearing as the most important thing in my life.

Parenthood is nothing short of astonishing. It's impossible to describe the love you feel for your own children. It goes beyond anything I have ever experienced before. Your children constantly remind you what it's all about. And I know that's a cliché, which we'll examine in a minute, but it's true.

Your children constantly remind you what it's all about.

At the time I was writing the original edition of this book, our boys, who were still very young, mostly spoke Italian. But then one of them started speaking to me in English. He said everything in English, and it was a miracle. My heart melted every time he said anything. A typical conversation:

'Daddy, what you doing, daddy?'

'I'm writing a book.'

'A book, Daddy? Where is it?'

'It's in here, inside here.'

'Inside the computer, Daddy?'

'Yes, and one day it will be a real book.'

'Can I see it, Daddy?'

'Yes, this is it, here.'

'Where, Daddy?'

'Inside here…'

So I suddenly had a gift that most parents don't have: one of my children speaking my own language proficiently. No 'cat', 'dog', 'daddy', 'mummy'… but 'Me been to the sea, Daddy, and play in tree, Daddy.' It was just amazing.

My children mean a lot to me. Maybe they mean everything to me.

So here we are, in a book about saying F**k It, talking about meaning causing pain and how things don't really matter as much as you think… and we bump up against the major irrefutable meaning of the children in our lives.

So let's get one thing straight: meaning is not wrong. Some things will always have meaning for you and for me. There's no need to feel bad that your children mean more than the world to you.

But children do give you an insight into your world of meaning. It's not possible to anticipate what it will be like to have children because it's impossible to see how much your world of meaning can change.

Just weeks after having your first child or children, you can't imagine what it was like *not* to have children. You can't imagine what you did with your time. You can't imagine why you used to worry about the things you used to worry about.

Having children is a major Perspective Machine. The things that mattered to you before, that had meaning to you, tend to humbly drop to their knees and start to shuffle apologetically out of the door, recognizing the awesome superior meaningfulness of the new arrivals.

Everything changes. And it demonstrates to us that meanings are not fixed. That they shift and change. Within one month of our boys being born, I said F**k It to a career that was previously important to me. It meant nothing any more. And I went with that.

So parenthood brings with it a natural level of F**k It. We naturally think F**k It to some of the things that previously mattered to us. Women previously lost in how they looked and what they wore are seen out at the local café in baggy jumpers with sick on their shoulders. Captains of industry with reputations for not suffering fools gladly are seen in sunny parks entertaining chuckling infants with coochycoochycoo noises and making peculiar faces and looking like, well, yes, like fools.

*Parenthood brings with it a natural level of F**k It.*

Being a parent gives you a unique insight into what it's like to say F**k It to lots of things in your life.

But what about parenting itself?

The first phenomenon of parenting is that everything is new and difficult. Looking after children is a very difficult job. And you don't get to go to college to learn the skills. You don't even get to go to evening classes. All you get is ante-natal classes (Why don't they change the name for a start? This can confuse people: 'Why should I go to classes run by people who are 'anti-natal'? I want to talk to people who are 'pro-natal', for Christ's sake.' It's not a good start, is it?).

These classes, though, only cover the pregnancy and birth. The best you get is a crash course in how to cope with the first day: i.e., changing nappies and how to hold your baby.

It's a bit like astronauts going to ante-take-off evening classes, and being taught everything about preparing for the take-off: 'Now, remember, the take-off could be difficult for all of you, you've got to help each other, look after one another. And don't forget to have your take-off bag ready just in case. Make sure you have your pyjamas, some spare underwear and your anti-gravitational sickness tablets. The main thing is to enjoy it. Take-off is a beautiful process and one you'll remember for the rest of your lives.'

Which is all very well and good, but what happens once they're up in space?

'Houston, can you read me? This is Apollo 21; repeat, Apollo 21.'

'Coming through loud and clear, Apollo 21. That was some take-off. We're all totally pissed on all that champagne down here, and are hugging, Apollo 21.'

'Read you, Houston. But, Houston...'

'Yes, Apollo 21...?'

'What do we do now?'

'Errmm, what do you mean, Apollo 21?'

'Well, there's, like, loads of, like, dials and switches and stuff, and every time I take my seat belt off I start flying all over the place, and I can't even have a crap without it starting to float around like some frickin' sci-fi movie… What the heck is going on up here, Houston?'

That's what it's like being a new parent. The only preparation you thought you were supposed to do for this post-birth period was to paint the nursery in bright colours and spend a fortune on stuff you don't really want.

After a couple of days of chaos you're on Amazon, looking for help. Fortunately, this has happened before, so someone thoughtful has written a book called *Fuck, I'm a Parent, What the Hell Do I Do Now?* and the pages are laminated so you don't ruin the book with piss, sick or liquid shit.

Fortunately, there's a book called Fuck, I'm a Parent, What the Hell do I do Now?

So you read the book and you feel out of your depth and this is what happens: Whenever we are unsure about something, a vacuum is created. And unless you live in a scientific laboratory where it's possible to create a vacuum in glass tubes by sucking out the air before sealing them and keeping them that way, then your vacuum is going to try to suck in stuff.

And, guess what? The whole world wants to fill your vacuum. Because everyone thinks they know about parenting. And they certainly think they know more than the tired-looking you does.

And you start to get advice from every angle.

You'll get advice from your parents, other mothers, people in the street, the medical profession, the government, even the Church.

I think giving unsolicited advice to new parents is a form of bullying: you catch someone at their most vulnerable and then bombard them with information.

But that's what vacuums do: they attract stuff that wants to fill them.

So it's a good idea to either seal your vacuum, or at least to put a filter on the gap that's sucking stuff in.

If you seal your vacuum, this is what you have to do: you have to realize that every single parent has gone through this uncertain patch of thinking they know nothing. So it's worth relaxing into this feeling. You then have to recognize that you do indeed know a good deal of the basics: you know how to change your baby, console your baby, feed your baby and dress your baby. And that – for a while at least – is all you need to know.

The rest, you can make up. Say F**k It to the barrage of advice and ideas about routine and sleeping patterns, and do what you think is best. The advice you will receive about a whole host of things 'baby' is just the advice that's in fashion at that moment. By next month it will have changed. And you risk subjecting your dearest to a theory that will soon be replaced by another theory.

*Say F**k It and do what you think is best.*

We both thought that – if in doubt – it's best to trust our instincts rather than an expert. And this is true in all areas of life: the best expert you'll ever find in the whole world is your own instinct.

If you prefer to put a filter on what is sucked into your vacuum of uncertainty, then please have some confidence in your filter. The filter is there to allow you to really check out what you're being told against what you feel is right.

If you're told that to stop your baby screaming in the evening you should be giving them Calpol, or Nurofen for Kids, and that doesn't feel right, then don't do it.

For new parents, illness in their young children can be frightening. But if we ever felt the need to get advice from doctors and they prescribed a drug, we would always ask, 'And what will happen if we don't use that drug?' The answer is usually something like, 'Oh, well, they may be in a little more discomfort for a couple of days.' Or, 'Well, it may take them a little longer to recover.' So, use your filter wisely.

The reason you are so anxious around your newborn – that they are so vulnerable – is the reason you have to be very careful what you put in their mouths. If in doubt, just trust yourself.

The bummer with trusting yourself, of course, is that, if you get it wrong, you can't blame someone else. But that's what self-responsibility is about.

Most people prefer to hand over responsibility for themselves and their children to other people so that they can blame someone else if something goes wrong.

But, in the end, blaming someone else won't make you feel any better. It won't get you anywhere; it will just make you feel stupid for trusting someone just because they were wearing a white coat.

If it helps, buy yourself a white coat and trust yourself.

The next thing about parenting will surprise you: most parents are scared of their children. Now I don't mean in a Damien out of *The*

Omen kind of way. I'm not suggesting that people are wondering whether they have spawned a messenger from the Underworld.

Most parents are scared of their children.

No, this is what I mean: fear derives from experience of – and therefore anticipation of – pain. And there's a lot of pain for parents around their children. There is clearly a lot of fear at the beginning. But we've talked enough about the beginning. Let's look at bringing up children once they've passed the involuntary pooing stage.

So to see why you'll be 'scared' of your children, just look at what they do that causes you pain:

* They go into wild, stroppy moods.

* They say 'no' when you ask them to do something.

* They misbehave in restaurants and other public places.

* They are always making a racket when you want some peace.

* They always want you to buy them something new.

So you develop, consciously or unconsciously, some fear around your children.

And this is what we do with that fear: we try to control our children. We impose discipline and 'boundaries' and we let them know that it's OK to do some things and not OK to do others. We force them to sit still in restaurants. We tell them that they have to be quiet when Daddy is reading his newspaper. We shout at them if they're in a mood until they stop being in a mood. And we threaten them when they do anything we don't want them to.

And the whole of society will support a disciplinarian approach to parenting. This is because everyone has this fear within them of what children might do.

It's as if children are monsters (how many times have you heard parents say, 'Oh, he's a little monster') who can turn round and eat us at any time. Children are beautiful, innocent and pure beings. Nothing a child does is wrong. The problem is our thinking that what they do is wrong. A child can literally do no wrong.

So, it's time (for you, at least) to say F**k It to this fear. And this is why:

* The less you try to control your kids, the more they'll take care of themselves.

* The less you discipline them, the better (generally) they'll behave.

This is a beautiful way to look after children because it's much less effort. If you've tried to teach your child or children how to sit still at the dinner table, you know how difficult 'controlling' children can be. Children are raw life-force. They sometimes want to run around and play, and they sometimes want to rest. That's what life does. There is night and there is day. There is rest and there is play. And with a child – like life – if you try to impose 'sitting still' on them when they want to move around, you're in for a struggle.

It's much easier to go with their rhythm than to try and impose yours.

When you get out of the way of children, they pass through things very quickly:

* A child left alone will soon stop shouting and be quiet again.

* A child left alone will soon stop crying and be happy again.

* A child left alone will soon stop racing around the restaurant and come and eat again.

And when I say 'alone' here, I do – of course – mean left without you trying to control them rather than literally 'alone'.

Have a go at doing less rather than more. If you're about to stop your child from doing something, or to tell them off, just hold yourself back and ask yourself whether it's worth waiting this time and seeing what happens if you don't.

If you take this course of less effort and intervention, you will invariably get some shit from other people. You'll get some looks in restaurants and in shops. And it's up to you where you decide that 'It's just their shit' and where they have a point (i.e., it must be darn disturbing here in the Savoy to have children leaping from table to table dressed as Spider-Man).

And if you're thinking, *Yeah, sure, sounds great in theory, but I'm sure it's a nightmare in practice*, listen to this: in the end, as parents, we don't 'know', we only *sense*. And all along, our sense as parents has been to let our children be. One summer when our boys were still at nursery, we attended a kite-flying party. As we sat with their teacher, she asked:

'What is it you do with Arco and Leone?'

'What do you mean?'

'What's the secret?'

'Go on...'

'Well, they're the best-behaved children in the school. We never have any problems. They even remind us when it's time to do things.'

Now this was a surprise to us. We have no attachment to them being 'well' or 'badly' behaved. Then, as now, we genuinely tried not to judge how they were in any way at all. And yet here they were, being praised for their 'good' behaviour.

So don't be scared of your kids; accept every part of them and let them be free.

You can control kids as much as you can control life. In other words, you can't (very easily).

Saying F**k It to parenting is giving up to what kids are. Just as saying F**k It to life is giving up to what life is. And the two things are practically the same. As kids are pure, unadulterated (hey, look at that word, un-adult-erated – cool) life energy. If you get used to saying F**k It to how your kids are, in all their playing, their sulking, their screaming and their tenderness, you will very quickly learn how to get used to saying F**k It to life.

SAY F**K IT TO SELF-CONTROL AND DISCIPLINE

OK, today I'm going to write the section on self-control and discipline.

But first I'm going to go for a walk and swim. Then I'll have a fruit breakfast. And I won't eat any bread today. And maybe I'll skip dinner tonight. Yes, I'll fast until tomorrow lunch. That should take a bit of this flab off. I was thinking that if I manage to swim every day until my birthday, maybe 50 lengths every day, I'll begin to look a bit better in, well, in my birthday suit.

Maybe that will become a bit tedious, though, doing the same thing every day. I know: I'll walk for an hour one day, then swim the next. And I'll give myself one day off a week. And I'm really going to try to get up before 7 a.m. every day from now on. And the first thing I'll do when I get up is have a cup of hot water with lemon. That's supposed to cleanse the liver. And maybe if I stick to just one glass of wine a night, that'll help cleanse the liver, too.

Shit. Almost forgot. What's this section about? Self-control and discipline? Phew, what do I know about that?

What I know is what you know: that our minds love the idea of self-control and discipline. We love the idea of improving, of bettering ourselves, of getting fitter and thinner, or smarter, or more accomplished.

And we think self-control and discipline are always the way. Well, our minds do, anyway. And the above little monologue is what typically goes on in my head. Even though I should know better by now, this is what my mind still gets up to. It just adores the idea of doing something at a certain time, consistently, every day, until some remarkable change has occurred.

So part of the F**k It here is that this stuff will probably be going on in your head *ad infinitum*. You may be lying in a hospital bed, aged 87, unable to move, surrounded by bags to catch your ones and twos, thinking: *If I could just get up and walk to the canteen once a day, I should be able to kick this thing. I could be in shape by Christmas. And I must stop eating that treacle tart, I must ask for the fruit salad instead. That way, I'll be cleansing my intestines and they'll get functioning again. And maybe I should ask Derek to bring in those French tapes — it'd be nice to learn a foreign language.*

Or maybe not. Maybe that's the good thing about age. Maybe we learn then what we should all learn much earlier on: it doesn't matter and it's not worth giving a shit.

For now, though, let's assume that your mind is going to be doing this stuff a good amount of the time. So say F**k It to it, and let it get on with it. Think of it as like a dog playing with a ball in the corner of your garden – just

*Say F**k It to your mind, and let it get on with it.*

let it play. If it shits on your begonias, then give it a good telling off, but otherwise, let it play.

With the rest of your mind, have a think about this:

The bugger with self-control and discipline is that it doesn't usually work that well, for most of us, anyway. (If you were in the SAS, I suspect you're very good at it and it's worked very well for you – why don't you skip this section? I'm sorry to have bothered you; please don't take offence, it's for weaker humans, really. Sorry.)

I don't have to tell you how this works. You'll be familiar enough with the numerous abandoned exercise plans, diets and evening classes.

Some people even make a business out of the fact that using our self-control and discipline doesn't work.

I've always wanted to look at the business plan of a big gym like Fitness First (I'm sad like that). I'd love to know what percentage of the people who join up in January they expect to still be coming to the gym by June. It's just a fantastic business idea. You get everyone to sign up to a monthly deal (and getting them to sign away a direct debit is the best way to do this) at the time when everyone's busy sorting out their plans to improve themselves for the year. And within one month, for 80 per cent of them, life has taken over and you will hardly see them for the rest of the year.

Just get a few more staff in for January, maybe hire a couple more rowing machines, and you're sorted. And you continue to take the £100 a month from their bank account.

The beauty – the absolute genius – of this business is that those 80 per cent of people don't get to mid-February and think: *Fuck me, I do this every year. I start with the best of intentions and within four weeks I never see the place again. I'll just cancel my membership today and never be so stupid as to go back there ever again. If I really feel like exercising I'll go outside and have a walk.*

What they all say is this: 'I must get back to the gym next week. I haven't been for a couple of weeks now. I shouldn't let it slip. I can't give in. All I need to do is go three times a week, and stop eating… blah, blah, blah.'

Very few people want to stop their £100 a month, because they don't want to admit they've failed. They don't want to admit they have no self-control or discipline. It's an expensive way to make yourself feel slightly better about not exercising. It's like buying a lie: 'I'm a member of a gym, so there must be something going on here.'

I'd prefer to buy a badge saying 'I exercise, you know'.

I'd prefer to buy a £1.50 badge saying 'I exercise, you know' that I could wear all the time. Now that's a cheaper way to buy lies.

I am happy to say that – years ago – I did say F**k It to gyms. The moment is very vivid for me. I was on one of those stepping machines. I'd been going this time for a couple of weeks, so I was getting rather good on this machine. I was improving on my previous time on every visit, and I'd soon be climbing up the equivalent of Mount Everest every lunch time.

Then, suddenly, as if there'd been a power-surge that had shot through the stepping machine and straight into my body, I looked around and saw everything with fresh eyes. It all just looked ridiculous: everyone indoors, pretending to be rowing or running or climbing hills or picking up logs. All watching MTV and trying to blank their minds to the absurd reality of what they were doing.

I pressed STOP.

As the two foot-bars of the stepping machine sank gently to the ground, I picked up my water bottle and walked calmly to the changing rooms. I enjoyed my shower, totally at one with myself in the knowledge that I would never set foot in such an absurd place again.

And I haven't.

This section is not sponsored by Fitness First, by the way. Even though I've used their name, I have not endorsed their cause. But I do admire their business plan.

Any attempt you make to control yourself – to impose discipline on yourself – can create some tension. It creates pressure that you usually can't live up to. And the disappointment you face when you can't live up to your own expectations is even more tedious than the frequency with which you let yourself down.

So just say F**k It to it all. Just do what the hell you want. Try not to set up daily tasks for yourself to get fitter or thinner or smarter (though we all still will, of course). Once you lose the tension of these self-imposed expectations, you will feel so much freer. And when you feel free, you will be more tuned in to what your body wants:

- ✱ You will feel like exercising when you feel energetic.

- ✱ You will feel like vegging out in front of the telly when you don't.

- ✱ You will feel like eating healthy food sometimes.

- ✱ You will feel like eating junk at other times.

- ✱ You will feel like stopping eating when you're full sometimes.

- ✱ And other times you will eat until you feel sick.

This is life. Give in to it.

The remarkable thing is that when you give in to the natural flow of life, you will most probably exercise more than you were doing when you were a member of a gym. And you will probably eat healthier food overall than when you were seeing that nutritionist. And you will probably eat smaller portions overall than when you were on some ridiculous diet.

This is how I live. I'm fitter. I'm the same weight. And I keep throwing myself into things like a child. It works for me.

But I don't want you to follow me. That will do you no good at all.

I want you to follow life.

SAY F**K IT TO PLANS AND GOALS

Plans and goals. A goal is the more anal twin brother of the plan. The plan dreams about what he wants to do; the goal then gets really focused and sets some deadlines for achieving these things. They're a very popular team, and lots of people like them and use their services.

Plans and goals are great

I've always been one for making plans and setting goals for myself. I've always been one for making lists of things I need to do and setting goals for different things in my life.

When you decide you want something, whatever it is, it's good to work out a plan for getting it, and to set up some deadlines for getting it done by. It works well.

The problem for a lot of people is that they don't really know what they want. They have vague desires — to 'do something creative' or 'earn more money' or 'be free' — but they can't really pin down precisely what it is that they want. So they drift from one thing to another, enjoying some moments and hating others, but never really finding fulfilment or success (whatever that means to them).

Not really knowing what you want in life is like going into your local DIY store and standing amid the huge aisles of stuff, not knowing what you came for. You wander around for a bit and then go to the information desk. You stand there until someone finally asks, 'Can I help you, sir?' And you look back at them blankly. 'Errrrmmmm… I was looking for… errrrmmm… I was hoping that… errrmmm… I don't really know what I want, actually… Could you recommend something, please?'

It sounds ridiculous. But that's exactly how a lot of people live their lives. And what happens in their lives is that the woman behind the information desk doesn't just get onto the store PA system and announce, 'Attention, all staff, we have L. Ooney at information; repeat L. Ooney at information. Can we have assistance, please?' No. She actually looks at them with sympathy and says, 'Well, if I was you, I'd start with some paint and a paintbrush. Give your place a bit of a smartening up, then maybe you can come back later for a drill and some shelves.'

When you don't really know what you want in life, the world can be very sympathetic and throw suggestions your way. But they often have no relevance to what you really need, because no one even knows what they want (like you).

It's hard to lead a successful life when you don't really know what you want.

This is why it's hard to lead a successful life (whatever that means to you) when you don't know what you want. A very vague message is sent out to the world, and you get only vague or inappropriate stuff back.

It's a different story, of course, if you go up to the information desk, get out your list and say: 'Good afternoon, could you please take me to find two-inch medial screws, lateral piping, the drill-generator section, and green envelope paint?' (Guess who doesn't do much DIY? Please bear with me.) Assuming that these things exist in the store, after dealing with L. Ooney just now, the assistant is happy to whisk you off to find everything you need.

And this is how the world works. When you're very focused on what you need, the world tends to help you get it.

Doesn't it say in the Bible, 'Ask and ye shall receive'? So, assuming that 'ye' means 'you' rather than some Scottish dude down the road, you're in for a good time if you start making plans (and goals).

Of course, the Bible also says, 'and the goat shall liveth with the man and the man shall be happy', and who needs goats to be happy nowadays? In this day and age, we can all be happy with our blow-up goats. They're far cleaner and, as long as they don't graze near thorn bushes, you're in for a trouble-free relationship.

So don't take everything the Bible says seriously. And that goes for what I say, too. Pick and choose. That's the way to wisdom.

To lead a successful life, then, it's a good idea to work out what you really want. Then get together some plans. Then set some goals. There are plenty of books on these things. So maybe your first plan could be to buy one of these books. And your first goal could be to buy it by Saturday and read it by the following Saturday.

But first read this next bit.

Plans and goals are rubbish

For exactly the reason that plans and goals are good for your life, they're a bummer, too. When you make a plan and set a goal, your life tends to move towards this point. You become very focused on what you're trying to achieve, and life does, too. What happens in this global attempt to reach your goal is that you block out all the other possibilities.

Imagine looking at a photograph on your computer of a crowded Trafalgar Square. It's a sunny day and everyone looks as if they're enjoying themselves. But you instantly start to home in on one detail: you use the magnifying facility to begin to focus on just one person – a man who is looking into one of the fountains. He seems lost and unaware of everything that's going on around him. And you continue to magnify down to his right hand. Where you find a tattoo of a peculiar symbol. You stare at that symbol and wonder what it must mean. You print this magnified picture and stick it on your wall to ponder on.

And this is what we do when we focus on something. No matter how fascinating the thing we focus on, we necessarily exclude all the rest of the stuff. You didn't pause to look at what other people were doing on that day. You didn't notice the reflection of light on the water of the fountain. You didn't spot the levitating dog show (a world premiere), and you didn't spot your wife in a passionate embrace with your best friend.

Every moment has infinite potential. Every new moment for you contains possibilities that you can't possibly imagine. Every day is a blank page that you could fill with the most beautiful drawings.

The problem with a plan is that you fill up the blank page of a new day with a 'to do' list before you get there. And if you're not careful, there's no room for anything else.

A plan narrows down the possibilities of the future.

A plan, especially a very focused one, narrows down the possibilities of the future to just a couple of things: that things either go to plan, or they don't (and you're disappointed). This is, of course, why many of us make plans: we are scared of infinite possibility and prefer to live with what we know and what we feel safe with.

But if you can say F**k It to this fear of possibility and unpredictability (see 'Say F**k It to Fear', pages 140–144), your life can really open up.

The way we live our lives is that we drag into each new moment the shit from the past and our limited expectations of the future. We drag into the present all our fears, our judgements, our hang-ups, our limits (of ourselves and others), and previously made plans.

Without any of these things, the moment is just open and ripe. We are free within a free and abundant world that responds to our freedom with unexpected gifts and blessings.

And yes, of course, this section has just contradicted the last. First, I'm wanting you to make plans, I'm even encouraging you to buy the book… then I'm telling you to abandon plans for a free life.

Trust me. I'm driving. And I know where we're going. So don't scream when I suggest…

Let's try taking our hands off the steering wheel

It's time for a story.

We are on holiday at Butlins in Skegness, on England's east coast. I am four. And I am in heaven. I am sitting inside a small 1930s-style car on a track, ready to go. Now, there are times in my life that I can remember exactly: what I was thinking, what I was feeling. And this is one of them.

So the ride begins and off we go. I am so excited. I am driving a car. Just like my dad drives his car, I am driving a car. And I'm hanging on to the steering wheel, ready to prove my abilities as a driver. I come to the first corner – a sharp right – and I carefully and precisely turn the steering wheel to the right. I come to the next corner – a left this time – so I turn the steering wheel to the left.

I am in bliss, I am driving. And I'm doing a good job by all accounts, given this is my first time out on the road/track.

But then a thought crosses my mind. A small thought at first. But it grows in size as I approach the next corner, another right. And I decide to put my thought to the test. As the moment arrives when I have to proficiently swing the steering wheel to the right, I proficiently swing it to the left. I see the risk of flying through the hedge and into the boating pond, but I take it anyway.

And what happens?

The car drives straight round the right bend, of course.

I am gutted. I am dizzy. And I start turning the steering wheel left and right in frustration. I am on a straight, and the steering wheel is turning freely in my hands with absolutely no effect.

I feel cheated beyond belief. Why don't they trust me? I can't understand it.

This feeling was soon to be repeated with the discovery that Santa Claus didn't exist. Then soon after that Jesus Christ was just a man with a beard and sandals from the past invented by men with beards and sandals in the present.

Most of us have been in that car for 30 or 40 or __ (please insert your age minus four or five) years. We've been driving round and round the track, diligently turning at every corner, thinking we're in control. We haven't yet tried taking our hands off the wheel. And we're now so tired that we're dropping off on the straights and shaking ourselves to wake up for the corners. We keep going because we think we have to keep going to stop the car from crashing.

It's time to rest, to put your feet up and enjoy the ride.

And now it's time to have a go at taking your hands off the wheel. And you'll soon find, like I did as a child, that the car drives itself. Only for you, given you're so knackered, you won't be disappointed at all, you'll be over the moon.

It's time to take your hands off the wheel of life. And you will indeed discover that it runs along quite happily without you doing a thing. It's time to rest, to put your feet up and sit back and enjoy the ride for a change.

It is a truly remarkable thing, this. And you'll only really get it when you do it. But the moment you stop trying to control and make things happen, everything just happens quite perfectly without you.

In fact, on the surface, little will change. You'll still go about your daily business. You'll still (apparently) be making decisions to do things. But you'll have this real sense that things are just happening.

In Taoism this is giving in to the natural flow of the Tao. In Scooby Doo, Shaggy would say, 'Go with the flow, man.'

The reality is that we actually have no choice in what goes on. We seem to have, but we don't.

This is just great news.

It means that we can just sit back and let things take their natural course. All the tension of 'I must achieve this and do this with my life' evaporates. Because the reality is that, whether you want it or not, it's going to happen (or not).

So making plans and goals is something you do or you don't do. You actually have no choice in the matter. You might end up getting the book on goal-setting and read it by next Saturday. Or you might not. You have no choice. Simply one of those two things will happen. And it's worth simply watching what happens with your life when you take your hands off the wheel.

I took my hands off the wheel a while back. And the book that I'd been trying to write for a couple of years… the book that I'd set up plans and goals for… well, it just started to write itself.

I write these words because I can't do anything else. No matter how hard I try, I can't do anything else. In fact, that's just a turn of phrase, because I'm not trying hard to do anything, or anything else. I am just living. And things are just happening very naturally. Including writing this very book. I'm enjoying writing it (for now at least), and I hope you're enjoying reading it.

Sometimes I make plans and goals, sometimes I don't. Sometimes I fulfil them, sometimes I don't. If I don't, sometimes I get upset. Sometimes I don't. This is the flow of life. And no matter what I do, it'll flow just the same.

Take my word for it.

This bit is like the bit in the Bible that says, 'Ask and ye shall receive', rather than 'shag goats and be happy.' Though if there are goats around and you end up shagging them, you can later console yourself that you had absolutely no choice in the matter anyway. That it just happened.

That, my goat-loving friend, is life.

So, say F**k It to goals and plans. If you're into them, you'll still have them. If you're not into them, you may start making them. But recognize that things are just as they are, no matter what you try to do with them.

Take your hands off the wheel and see what happens. And just to make life even more interesting, press down on the accelerator at the same time.

SAY F**K IT TO WANTING THE WORLD TO BE A BETTER PLACE

It's impossible to separate spiritual people from people who want the world to be a better place. Sure, there are plenty of people who aren't spiritual who also want the world to be a better place. But there aren't many spiritual people who aren't interested in it. So we're all working for good to triumph over evil, for peace to reign over all, to eradicate hunger and terrorism.

But haven't you noticed something?

No matter how hard people try, the apparent balance between 'good' and 'evil', between 'peace' and the opposite, fighting and war, always remains pretty much the same. There have always been 'good' people. And there have always been 'bad' people. The effects of good action in the world have been phenomenal. And so have the effects of bad action. The latter just tends to get more news. In fact, the latter tends to get all the news. Consequently, we tend to think that the world is generally 'bad' and we've got to make it a better place.

> *No matter how hard people try, the apparent balance between 'good' and 'evil' remains pretty much the same.*

And, just as an aside on this news thing, there's a newspaper that sets out to redress the news imbalance: it only gives you positive news. In fact, it's called *Positive News*. It does what it says on the tin. Have you read it? If you haven't, try to find a copy. It's available in all good vegan newsagents. Read it. And see if you can stay awake. You'll be reaching for your regular doom-filled daily before you can say 'paedophile crack dealer in terrorist plot'.

And I'm not dissing all those who pray for peace, fight evil and try to beat the bad guy. I'm also not dissing all those who pray for destruction, fight good and try to beat the good guy. They will both go at each other, tooth and nail, for as long as there are humans.

Sometimes it will look like the good guy's winning. Sometimes the bad guy. In the end, it all works out the same: they balance each other out over time.

So here's the thing: let's recognize that good will never win out over bad, or vice versa. Let's accept things as they are... just exactly as they are right now. Let's say F**k It to the battle. It really doesn't matter. The news is the same every day. Just with different names. It's boring.

So just feel what it's like to give up the battle (whichever side you're on). You're not going to win. You're not going to make a difference. Because the final score is always a draw (which is great if you're into the pools). Give up your desire for the world to be a better place, and do the pools instead.

What does it feel like? Yes, again, it feels like you're relaxing. It feels like you're lying back. You lose your tight grip on life. You lose your desire for things to be other than they actually are.

> *Resigning yourself to things as they actually are is a real blast.*

Finally resigning yourself to things as they actually are is a real blast. This is the blast of saying F**k It.

Like everything else that you do, once you start saying F**k It, the effect is peculiar. Once you give up wanting the world to be a better place, you may well start actually doing something that has an apparent effect in the world.

It's a bugger, isn't it? But as you're probably beginning to get, it does seem to be true. If you're not beginning to 'get', just F**k It anyway.

SAY F**K IT TO CLIMATE CHANGE

How are you dealing with the problem of climate change? A problem created by our putting so much pressure on the systems of this 4.5-billion-year-old planet that it is getting rapidly more sick.

My guess is that you're exhibiting (like all of us have always done) one of these responses: 'fight' or 'flight'. In this case, rather than facing or running away from tigers, 'fight' means that you're bringing your full awareness to the threat, thinking about what it means and what we can personally do in the face of it; 'flight' is when we run away from the problem by denying that it exists (it does, by the way), by despairing that there's nothing we can do now (there is, by the way), by 'doing our bit', then getting on with our regular lives.

Even though the 'flight' option seems absurd, most people are still in that camp.

It is actually very difficult to bring your full awareness to the issue of climate change. One problem is that most of us don't have the imagination to realize fully what's going on. We're like that frog. When he was popped in boiling water, he jumped out, and when he was popped in lukewarm water, and then slowly boiled, he stayed right there and boiled to death.

Well, the water's beginning to boil.

So what can we do? Say F**k It to Climate Change, of course. And in this context, F**k It means relaxing. After all, it's the panicky fear that switches us to 'flight' mode. So relax. Breathe deeply (even if the air around you is polluted). Relax and then decide to have the courage to face this one. Face it every day. Think deeply about what's going on and what your place can be in dealing with climate change.

As you face the problem, don't feel obliged to do anything at all. That feeling of obligation is like leaving the window open and letting that pesky tension get back in. Don't let me tell you what to do. Don't let anyone pressure you into doing something. Don't feel guilty about what you've done or haven't done… or what we as humankind have done or haven't done.

Say F**k It and start afresh today: relaxed, pressure-free, guilt-free — and then ACT. Act big-time. Act small-time. But act.

If the whole thing still sends you into despair and flight mode, think about this: at a time in the history of humanity when we have the technology to blow each other to smithereens (and take the rest of the world with us), this could be the one thing that binds us all together. The natural reaction to our industrialization (in the form of natural disasters) could be so devastating that we have no choice but to put aside differences and tackle the problem together. We'll probably realize that we are bound to each other, just like we'll realize that we're bound to this Earth and its systems.

At the moment just before we all go down, we'll probably realize that we're all one, that all is one — just like all the gurus and teachers have all been going on about for so long. Ironic, really, as it's the perception of separation (from each other and from nature) that has got us here in the first place.

*Please shout F**k It and finally do something about our sick Earth.*

So please grab the hand of the person next to you, shout F**k It and finally do something about our sick Earth.

SAY F**K IT TO YOUR ISSUES

I had a very English upbringing. English, and Christian to boot.

So we were always a happy Christian family with no problems, conflicts or issues. At least, that's what we liked to think.

Underneath the surface, of course, was bubbling the whole range of human emotion and experience: unhappiness, anxiety, jealousy, desire, pain, heartache, grief, fear and so on. But there was no room within the family for any of these 'shadow' sides. We all had to be happy and content, good examples of Christian living. That's not to say that we weren't happy and content and joyful and loving. We were. But we weren't *just* that.

I knew this as I was growing up. I knew that things didn't feel right. That there wasn't the space for 'all' of me, just one side of me.

In adulthood I considered what was going on in this dynamic. And this is where I got to:

It is a very natural human impulse to move towards pleasure and to avoid pain. It is, in fact, very healthy to accentuate the positive and reduce the negative. The problem occurs when the pain is already within us. When the 'negative' is already within our cells. No matter how much we avoid it, it doesn't go away. In fact, it simply tries to be heard more, the more we ignore it.

What seems to happen is that pain tries to let us know it needs listening to in different ways. And one way it tries is through illness.

> *Pain tries to let us know it needs listening to in different ways.*

In the world of holistic healing, every illness has an emotional source. So there needs to be a healing of the emotional source of an illness before physical healing can take place. In the world of therapy and healing, it is recognized that you need to look inside at the pain to move on.

The impulse to take this journey usually only comes when some pain inside you has become too great to bear. Or your illness has become too painful.

Life is very beautiful in that way. The natural impulse to avoid pain is naturally counterbalanced by a pain that can't be ignored. And you begin your journey into the healing of pain.

I have been involved in the world of therapy for a long time, and a lot of healing does occur. But my observation is that the journey into healing itself can become addictive. Once you've summoned up the courage to deal with pain, and you've faced different levels of pain within yourself, the process of cleansing pain can become a constant one:

* We go through emotional therapy processes to look at past pains in order to try to heal them.

* We go through physical therapy processes to try to cleanse the body of toxins and pains.

* We go through energetic therapy processes to try to clear the energetic system in our body and release blocks.

And it's easy to start to obsess about what we have to clear. So:

* We obsess about the traumas we haven't yet dealt with.

* We obsess about the aches and pains and discomforts we still feel.

* We obsess about our unclear energy systems.

And the journey into healing, into wholeness, becomes an endless one.

Add to this other concepts, such as:

* the cleansing of karma from previous lives

* the freeing of spiritual intrusions from your soul body

* the pursuit of immortality

— and you're in for one hell of a journey.

A journey that could last not just this lifetime, but many lifetimes to come (and this is what some people actually think).

Cor blimey, what an effort! How utterly tedious.

You see, the world responds to whatever desire we have. If we desire to go on a 'journey' of healing, the world will offer us endless ways to keep us occupied on that journey.

Just at one very simple level – your own issues around your childhood, say – you could go on trying to heal them forever (and a lot of people charge a lot of money trying to 'help' you do just that).

Yes, my friends, it's time to say F**k It to your issues. Say F**k It to your journey into healing and wholeness. I was on that journey, and I did find that it was going on a bit. That underneath every issue and pain was another one. Then another one. Then another one. There is a bottomless well of pain if you really fancy taking the leap.

So, thus far, we have two paradigms, two ways of seeing life and our journey through it:

* to focus on the pleasure, and ignore the pain, at whatever cost

* to focus on the pain, and forget about all the pleasure.

There is, of course, another way. A way where we accept that life is just a dance between pleasure and pain. If you ignore pain, it doesn't go away. If you try to heal pain, there's still more there. Because pain is a part of life.

Life is pain and pleasure in equal measure.

Life is pain and pleasure in equal measure.

And a funny thing can happen. When you finally accept this, you can stop naming these things, too. When you give up your obsession with clinging to pleasure (paradigm 1), or chucking out the pain (paradigm 2), you can just live and experience. You can stop moving towards something and moving away from something else.

You can just be.

You recognize that life is just, well, life.

SAY F**K IT TO WHAT OTHER PEOPLE THINK OF YOU

Why we care about what other people think of us

Some of us care a lot about what other people think of us. And it seems a very basic urge as we're growing up to seek approval. I saw it when my children were young: they loved to be seen doing things, to be laughed at when they did funny things, to be congratulated when they did something special. If we give children the attention and the approval they are seeking, they tend to develop a sense of self-worth or self-esteem. In other words, by fulfilling their need for approval from the outside world, they tend to develop a sense of self-approval.

And it seems that, as we grow up, we are defined by the level of self-approval that we have. If our earlier need for approval was not fulfilled and we therefore have a low level of self-approval (please feel free to interchange the word 'self-esteem'), then we are likely to continue wanting approval from the outside world.

If a loving environment in childhood created high levels of self-approval, then we are less likely to be constantly seeking approval from others as adults.

Of course, between these two extremes lie most of us. We're not rabid attention-seekers, but we are sensitive to how people view us.

The other aside here is that I have no particular judgement about this either. It is a subject that has always fascinated me. Particularly in regard to success. Those with low self-approval can be driven to high levels of success because of their exaggerated need for the external approval that they probably never got as children.

Imagine the hyper-driven, mega-successful film or pop star who appears to have endless energy for new roles, and new ways with which to woo an ever-larger world audience. Think of someone like Marilyn Monroe. She had the world at her feet. She even had the president of the world's superpower at her feet (well, maybe not her feet), yet she is famous for her insecurity, self-doubt and lack of self-approval.

Go the other way and young adults with high levels of self-approval might lack the drive to 'achieve' anything… they are content to just bumble along, enjoying life.

We care, then, what other people think of us, first of all because we want their approval: more so when we lack approval for ourselves.

We are taught that it matters what other people think of us.

We are also taught that it matters what other people think of us. We are taught that to live successfully in society, we should be respectful to other people, we shouldn't upset anyone, we should help people and we should do as we're told (to take an example of a very early teaching that we receive).

We learn that it matters what other people think of us because that's how everyone else is. That's how your parents probably were, that's how your teachers were, that's how your friends were.

131

Another reason it matters to us what other people think of us is that we tend not to know what we actually want. If people have very clear aims and goals in life, they tend to get on with fulfilling those goals no matter what. Because they know what they want, and are confident in achieving it, they have the strength to deflect all the different critical views that come their way: you must spend more time doing your homework; you must think about doing a proper job; you are just a waster… etc. When we know what we want, what people think of us can become less important in the pursuit of that goal.

The iffy side of caring what other people think of you

Caring what other people think of you clearly works for some people. For others, it constrains and narrows their lives. If you're surrounded by safe, conservative people – and you care what they think – you are unlikely to move beyond the safe, conservative boundaries that they place on their own lives. No matter how you feel – no matter what your desires – you will feel blind fear at the thought of doing things that upset those people around you:

* This is how gay people end up in straight marriages.

* This is how talented singers end up as accountants.

* This is how comedians end up as barristers.

* This is how barristers end up as bar staff.

We all have bundles of potential. And the iffy side of caring what people think is that you might well end up doing only the safe things that they want you to do. Everyone simply imposes their own fears and regrets on everyone else: when individuals limit themselves, they can be certain to go around limiting other people (usually in a very moral fashion) to try and make up for the deep pain they feel for not doing what they should have done.

Which brings us on to:

Other people are never being personal

When you really care what other people think of you, you tend to take everything personally. It's possible to develop a somewhat twisted view of the world when you really care what other people think. You crave approval, and when you get it, you're happy. When you're the life and soul of the party, or the centre of attention, you're happy as Larry (I'm not quite sure which Larry, but let's hope he was a happy fellow, otherwise that bit won't work).

But anything that smacks of anything but approval throws you off. If someone neglects to say 'Good morning' to you, you wonder why. If you aren't lauded for your new report, you get down (I don't mean in a funky way, but in a depressed way). If that attractive woman/man doesn't look at you, you start to wonder whether you're ugly. A shop assistant is rude and off-hand to you and it makes you furious. A car cuts you up on the motorway and you chase after it, in the mood to kill.

Your somewhat paranoid view of the world – where you start to take everything personally – can become ridiculously exaggerated. I know people whose whole life revolves around fighting back against the rude and ignorant people (strangers) around them.

So it may be that the people who neglect to say 'Good morning' to you are being personal: they may well not like you. But it's very unlikely that the ones cutting you up on the motorway have singled you out for some rough treatment because they don't like the look of your face (or your bum-per).

But the truth is, even those who from almost every perspective seem to be being personal with you, are not being personal.

Let's look at an example. Cheryl is a news presenter for a local news channel. She presents the news with Keith, who is 10 years older. One day Keith sits Cheryl down to air a few 'truths', and he gets personal: 'Look, Cheryl, this is hard to say, but I think I need to say it, and maybe it will help you in the end. The thing is, I've seen the way you are with the other men in the studio. Without being rude, it seems that you're working your way through them. It's not that there's anything wrong with it, of course, it's just that it doesn't look good. It's not professional. And to get to the top of this profession, you need to be professional. So, Cheryl, I'd hold back a bit. Sit pretty, hold back and you'll be fine.'

The reality is that Cheryl is single and has simply been out with a couple of guys in the studio. She's never really had a long-term partner, and the idea that anyone would ever think of her as a 'slag' appals her.

So what Keith says hits her hard. It was personal and she feels it deeply personally. She is very upset and spends a lot of time crying.

This is a translation of what Keith was *really* saying:

'Look, Cheryl, this is hard to say, but I think I need to say it, and maybe it will help you in the end. (Look, Cheryl, I wish I could say something that I really need to say, but I'm scared of what you'll think of me.) The thing is, I've seen the way you are with the other men in the studio. (And it's driving me madly jealous.)

'Without being rude, it seems that you're working your way through them. (Why the hell haven't you thought about me? I'm the one who loves you.) It's not that there's anything wrong with it, of course (it's wrong, I hate it, because I want you to be mine), it's just that it doesn't look good (it's driving me crazy). It's not professional. (I've got to think of something to put you off these men.)

'To get to the top of this profession, you need to be professional. (Though if you'll have me, I'll help you get there anyway.) So, Cheryl, I'd hold back a bit. (With them, and notice me… ME.) Sit pretty (you are so beautiful, Cheryl), hold back and you'll be fine (hold me and you'll be fine. I love you).'

What upset Cheryl so much was actually a serenade. All the negative words came from Keith's fears and insecurities and judgements.

And when people are apparently 'personal' with you, they're usually venting their own negative emotions. It may be that you mirror their shadow-side: the part of them that they can't admit to. It may simply be that they're jealous of you for some reason. It may be that they're simply in a bad mood and just want to take it out on someone. But the fact is that practically every time people get personal with you, it's almost always more about them than it is about you.

So it's not worth taking anything personally, because it's unlikely to be about you. Of course, if you weigh 20 stone and you go and sit on your neighbours as a joke and they start to suffocate and splutter, 'Get off me, you fat bastard, you're going to kill me, you lardy moron,' then it *is* personal, it *is* about you, and they *have* got a point. And I'd get off them and go home and make yourself feel better by eating a tub of Häagen-Dazs in front of *Flashdance*.

You can't keep everyone happy

If it really matters to you that other people approve of you, you will invariably come up against one hell of a bummer fact: you can't please all of the people all of the time.

It is a fact. No matter how much you bend over backwards for people, you'll always disappoint people, upset people and downright piss them off sometimes.

This is because everyone is different. Every single person has a unique GFUC, or Genetic Fucked-Up Code. Most people are fucked up, but their fuck-ups are completely different. Which means that –

It's not worth taking anything personally, because it's unlikely to be about you.

even with one person – as much as you try to please them, you're going to tap into one or two of their fucked-up qualities and get slaughtered for it.

The fact is that – even when you really want to – you can't keep that many people happy for that much of the time. That's because people aren't that good at being happy. And they're not that happy to simply 'approve' of other people. They prefer to find things in you that piss them off... things in you that they think are inferior to the things in them... this makes them feel (temporarily) a little bit better.

But – if you care what other people think – it makes you feel terrible.

Do you want to make everyone unhappy?

If your early attempts to get approval from parents and the people around you failed big-time, there's a chance you'll be mightily pissed off. And this tends to really hit the world when you're a teenager.

You've spent so long wanting people to like you – without anyone saying anything nice to you – that you decide to hit back. This is you saying to the world: 'OK, I wanted your attention. And if you're not going to give it to me for all the good things I did, then you'll bloody well give it to me now. You'll not be able to ignore me, you sad bastards. Because now the bomb is going to go off.'

This is when things go tits-up. This is when boys and girls and men and women cause havoc and end up achieving their aim: they get attention.

And they end up making everyone scared and unhappy. All they're doing is asking for love… it's just got a bit messed up along the way.

So, by talking about caring less about what people think of you, I don't mean growing a Mohican, spraying 'Police are wankers' on your dad's car or setting light to the church hall.

Saying F**k It to things will really wind people up

It's worth thinking about how much you care about what other people think of you, not least because the moment you start to say F**k It to various things in your life, you'll really start to wind people up. And it's worth being ready for this.

Before you started reading this book, you were involved in a conspiracy of meaning with everyone around you. You and everyone around you gave the relatively usual meanings to various things in your life: you will have had shared experiences of what mattered. You also fit perfectly into your place in the world: your parents expect you to be one thing, and expect certain behaviours (related to how you view different meanings), so do your friends, so do your colleagues at work and your boss, and so does the rest of the world, including the government (it continues to expect that a person like you regards it as important to pay taxes, for example).

The moment your world of meanings starts to shift a little is the moment you start to upset this balance. The moment you start to free yourself from your normal attachments and meaning by saying F**k It to things, is the moment people will start to get pissed off with you.

This is because all the other people around you, deep down, know that their myriad meanings are the cause of all their problems. It's OK to stay within this pain when everyone else is doing the same thing. But as soon as you show that there's possibly another way, they'll get very jealous. Something deep in them will see the freedom they've always craved and they'll want it. But they won't come politely to your door or desk and ask you if you could be so kind as to share whatever wisdom you've received; they'll kick back and criticize you and think you're terrible.

This is because anyone who shows any signs of real freedom reminds everyone else what a prison they're living in. And prisons, especially nowadays, seem to be darn difficult things to get out of.

> *Your freedom reminds everyone else what a prison they're living in.*

Let's say that you've really examined your feelings and issues around death, and that death now holds less weight for you. In many senses you've said F**k It to death. Death means less to you. When someone close to you dies, you go through some grief that you can't spend time with them any more. You remember the good times you had together.

But this lasts a relatively short time. And you are soon back to normal life. Those around you, and your family, think your behaviour is strange and callous. You don't get involved in the drama of the death. You haven't fulfilled the expected quota of grief demonstration.

And people criticize you.

The fear of death creates an expectation of reaction. If you don't fulfil this expectation you will be criticized. In the end, people simply take it personally: 'Well, you don't really seem to have cared that much about this person; is that how you feel about me? Is that how quickly you'll forget me once I've died?'

When the power of a meaningful world begins to diminish for us, we challenge everyone whose worlds are still so meaningful. So the moment people do start to react to how you are, smile and say quietly, F**k It.

It's time to say F**k It to what people think of you.

Approval is like anything else in this life: it can cause pain if it has a lot of meaning for you – if you're attached to it.

This is not to say that if people are prostrating themselves at your feet and telling you how wonderful you are, you shouldn't enjoy it. But if you believe you won't be happy until every last damn citizen of this planet is worshipping you, then you're in for a hard time.

So start saying F**k It to what people think of you.

If you can be arsed, you can do a little exercise:

Speak out (or write down) what you think other people think of you, and then follow it with a big F**k It:

* Aunt Mabel thinks I steal her sweets. F**k It.

* Gale Cranthorpe thinks I'm after her sister. F**k It.

* Mr Jessica thinks I'm lazy. F**k It.

* God thinks I'm a hopeless sinner. F**k It.

It really doesn't matter what people think of you. Just like nothing really matters.

* Enjoy going your own way.

* Enjoy zigging when others are zagging.

* Enjoy doing something in public you wouldn't normally do (this is not an invitation to flash, by the way).

* Enjoy telling people the truth for a change rather than just trying to keep them happy.

* Enjoy getting into work late if you normally arrive on time.

* Enjoy being rude to someone who pisses you off.

It's time to care less about what others think of you.

It's time to say F**k It and feel what it's like to be free.

SAY F**K IT TO FEAR

Fear and love

There are two apparently opposing forces that govern our lives. No, not good and evil. Love and fear.

That's right: the opposite of love is not hate, but fear.

We tend to operate in either of these two modes.

We can either embrace and love life – this is called the *libido*. And I like this word. Mainly because most people think it's about how high your sex drive is. So when you say, 'Yes, I have a high libido,' they think you could be a sex addict and suggest you should be put in a dark room with Michael Douglas. But libido is simply a love for life. If you have a high libido, you simply have a great love – even lust – for life.

And Lust for Life – as well as being a great song by Iggy Pop – is a great thing to have. When we go out to life with love, we are completely open.

The opposite mode is when we are in fear (rather than in love). In fear we close to life. In fear we go inside and hide. We want to retreat and block ourselves off from experiences.

Most of us are constantly moving between these two modes. It's a bit like a game of snakes and ladders. We bound up the ladders of love, sucking up life for all that it is. Then we hit scary snakes and slide down them as we retreat from life. It's a good analogy, because one thing that a lot of us are bloody scared of is snakes. Which takes me on to my next point rather neatly.

It is rational to be afraid of some things

There are things in life that it's understandable to be afraid of. A fear of snakes and spiders is quite natural, as – depending on where you are in the world – both can be very dangerous. If you have an innate fear of snakes, then when you see one, adrenaline will start to pump and make you more able to act quickly and appropriately.

There are things in life that it's understandable to be afraid of.

Some people have a 'fear' of blood. Again this is quite natural, because if we ever see bright red arterial blood, it means things are pretty serious.

The problem with even these very natural 'fears' is that they can get out of hand. A fear of blood can lead you to faint at the sight of blood rather than act quickly to stem its flow.

I prefer the idea of being aware around dangers rather than being scared. And this is indeed what *beware* means… to *be aware*. It is important to be aware of how dangerous driving a car is, but not to be scared of driving. It is helpful to be aware that crossing a busy road carries a risk, but not to be scared of crossing roads. It is wise to be aware that skiing down a black slope in a blizzard has potential problems, but not to be scared of skiing.

At a very natural level, we become scared of things that have the potential to cause us pain, even death: and this is the origin of fear in us.

The origin of fear

'Fear' in us is not just one lump. It is a sackful of stuff that we have built up over our lives. And fear grows from the experience of pain. When we experience pain we – very naturally – do not like it and we do not want to experience it ever again. So the experience of pain then becomes a fear.

Fear grows from the experience of pain.

For example, we might be quite happy chopping up carrots with our favourite sharp knife every day. Until the day that we take the end of a finger off. The pain creates a fear of using sharp knives. We have just added another bit of fear to our sack.

You might be quite happy speaking in meetings at work. Until the day that you're feeling a little bit under the weather, and – halfway through making some brilliant point – you completely lose your track. You stumble and fall. You have no idea what you were saying. And you apologize and fluff your way to a halt. It's embarrassing beyond belief. And the pain stays with you for the rest of the day. Come the next important meeting and you suddenly find you're afraid to talk. One more screwed-up ball of fear for your sack.

The problem with life – as we now know – is that anything that means something to us has the potential for pain. So it's possible to develop fears for anything and everything. Some people are scared of falling in love because of the pain they've previously experienced in love. People are scared of doing what they want to do because it previously went wrong for them. Some people are scared of leaving their own house because of some pain they previously experienced outside the house.

Let's not forget that this process is natural. Even the apparently extreme expansion of the fear sack is quite natural. It is based on a principle that we all take part in: feeling pain and then being scared.

This is why age often brings with it a heightened sense of fear. Time for some people simply offers more opportunities to experience pain and develop fear. This is one reason why older people can be very scared and timid.

Yet we all know people who seem to be absolutely fearless. They are adventurous and confident and are out in the world loving their lives. Yet they are likely to have experienced as much 'pain' as anyone: in fact, they have probably experienced *more* pain, given they were more likely to have been flying down that black slope in the blizzard or overtaking on a corner.

And this is – I think – what happens. Our fear quotient is dependent not on how much pain we encounter – but how we *respond* to pain. Let's go back right to the beginning. To our birth. Just to reinforce the idea that life means pain and pleasure, our birth is painful (and pleasurable). Our first experience of the world outside the womb is of pain. It's hard to get our first breath. There's no liquid like we're used to. It's probably very light. And, most likely, not as warm as we'd like.

But it's not the pain of the birth itself that will leave us the lasting impression, but the *environment* in which it is felt. The same level of actual pain will have a different effect depending on how people in the room respond to it. If you are born into a room full of fearful, panicky people, it's going to be a very different effect from being born into a room of calm, loving people.

This is the way we're taught early in our lives about how to interpret pain. When we experience pain, the way the people around us respond to it then teaches us to respond in a similar way. If we're sick as a child and those around us feel anxious and afraid, then we learn that this is the way to respond to such pain. If we cut or burn ourselves as a child and an adult makes a massive deal about it, then we learn that this is the way to respond to such pain.

This is how many of us 'learn' to respond to pain in whatever form. This is our inheritance. Our parents were probably 'taught' their response to pain by their parents, and so they pass it straight to us.

It comes down to this: we either learned that it was OK and safe to be in pain. Or that it wasn't.

It's safe to be in pain

Most of us were taught that it is neither OK nor safe to be in pain. And this is what generates the growing sackful of fear that we live with and through.

So it's time to start looking at how you are around pain. You'll probably see that you panic a little (or a lot) around any pain. Whether it's cutting your finger or getting the flu, being told something you didn't want to hear or getting bad news over the phone, you will probably notice that you panic.

So the first thing to tell yourself is that there's nothing to panic about. I've played the game of affirmations before, and they can be very powerful. This was one of my favourites: 'I am safe, no matter what I'm feeling.'

> *Tell yourself: 'I am safe, no matter what I'm feeling.'*

It's beautiful. Because it's a self-cancelling affirmation. You're clearly *not* feeling safe, but you tell yourself that you are, even if you're feeling that you're not.

It's worth trying.

Given that our response to pain is the heart of our own fear, this chapter could more aptly be called Say F**k It to Pain. Because as soon as you crack pain, you'll crack fear.

So start saying F**k It to pain. When you respond to pain, you are only acting out a conditioned response. And all conditioned responses are reversible. When you encounter any pain, counter your immediate response by just saying F**k It.

You are safe. In the end, nothing matters. Give in to pain and you can give in to life.

And as you start to say F**k It to pain, you'll notice a couple of things. Your fear for things will begin to evaporate. And this fear will be replaced by libido: the love and lust for life.

This process has real momentum: the less you fear, the more you crave doing things that would have previously scared you. And the more that you do, the more that you get out there, the more you realize you can do and the more you realize there is to do.

Before long you'll be playing the guitar in Leicester Square, going white-water rafting in Canada, dumping your job and writing a film, or simply telling Hunky Hugh in accounts that you think he's really hunky and would he like to go to see a film (that you've written).

> *Say F**k It to pain and you'll be saying F**k It to fear.*

So, say F**k It to Pain and you'll be saying F**k It to Fear.

SAY F**K IT TO BEING UPTIGHT

I've just got back from the local post office (remember, we're in Italy). As I was waiting in line, there were two customers in front of me and two at the desks, and three members of staff behind the desks, two of them dealing with customers, the other doing some paperwork.

And the one doing the paperwork was clearly really miffed with the employee next to her: 'I can't come here in the morning and have to deal with this kind of problem; it's not up to me,' she said to him. The guy was giving as good as he was getting: 'That happens to be your job, so why on earth can't you just do it?'. 'Well, it was never made clear to me that I would have to deal with this kind of problem...' And so on.

These two were not holding back, despite the fact there were customers present, and another member of staff. They were just bickering, like an old couple. Nothing vicious, just gentle bickering. And it made me feel uncomfortable. I couldn't understand why they didn't just hold it back; save it until later. But there seemed to be no awareness that this wasn't a great thing to be doing: having a public argument, especially in front of customers. I looked around. No one else – customers or staff – seemed uncomfortable: I don't know whether they'd even noticed what was happening. And then I remembered something: we're in Italy, and I'm English.

In England, we *do* hold it back. We're polite even when we're seething. We save it until later, and that later often never comes. We keep it in and push it down. Not so here in Italy. I've lived here for years now, but it clearly hasn't sunk in at a deeper level that this is what people do.

Years ago, I'd constantly implore Gaia and her mum to stop arguing. They'd pause, look at me in surprise, and say: 'We're not arguing, we're just talking'. Well, it bloody well looked like arguing to me: raised voices, overt gesticulations.

But then I saw that people here do indeed raise their voices and gesticulate dramatically, even when they're just talking about the weather (which they do, it's not just us Brits. Although they talk more about food. Brits talk incessantly about the weather, while Italians talk incessantly about food).

So, those two post office employees were having a barney, and they weren't bothered about who heard it. And the people who heard it weren't bothered about hearing it. It didn't feel great to me, but maybe it was: she was telling him that she wasn't happy, he was listening, and then saying his piece, too. Clear, honest communication. Nothing held back. They didn't come to blows. They'll probably work it out.

I'm getting used to this kind of communication (though clearly not *completely*, or this morning's episode wouldn't have made me feel uncomfortable). And when I go back to the UK, which I do fairly regularly, I'm struck by how much people hold back when they're talking. We communicate, generally, in a polite way, even when we're trying to express something difficult.

We'd never say something difficult *outright*, so we try to make it clear without actually *saying* it. Yes, I know, madness. Therefore, we have become adept at reading between the lines of any conversation. Here's an example:

You get on well with the couple next door and their children, but the son plays loud music late into the evening and it disturbs you. If you're British, though, the next time you are invited over to their house for a glass of wine, you don't just come out with it: 'Your son's music is a little too loud for us in the evening… it's fine during the day, but it's too much in the evening. Could you ask him to keep it down, please?'

No, first you spend a long time deliberating over how to broach the subject. Then you work out ways to drop hints into the conversation. You might, for example, be talking about some other family and refer to their son as a tearaway who's up all night taking drugs and terrorizing the neighbourhood with his loud music. By exaggerating the story, you make it clear that you're not talking about *them*, but it will certainly make them wonder whether their son's music is a problem for you.

Or you invent something. Maybe you say that you've been suffering from headaches recently, and that you've become very sensitive to noise – so much so that you can't bear your daughter doing her piano practice. When the neighbours say, as they probably will, 'Oh, I hope our son's music is not disturbing you,' you'll even exclaim, 'Oh no, I wasn't saying *that* (even though you were), I'm just finding any loud noises difficult.' Your neighbours then get the point and talk to their son.

It is madness, but it's how it's done. It means, though, that you're always wondering what people are actually trying to say. You never know whether something is genuine or just some padding to something that's more difficult to express.

In business, there's even a dreadful expression for this: the 'shit sandwich'. If you have something difficult to say to someone – such as, 'You're not doing well enough' – you start off by saying some nice stuff about them: 'We're all very happy with how you're getting on.' That's the first slice of bread. Then you hit them with the shit: 'That said, we think you could do better in this area.' Then you complete this charming sandwich with another slice of soft bread: 'But, overall, we're all very happy with you.' Bullshit.

What this means is that no one trusts what anyone says any more. When someone pays you a compliment, you're always waiting for the 'but, that said' that comes afterwards.

This means that the UK is, generally, more uptight than somewhere like Italy. Because it's hard to say stuff openly, we either don't say it (suppress it), or we struggle to find a way to say it. And on the receiving end, we struggle to work out what the hell everyone's trying to say to us.

For example, you pop into the baker's one morning and are greeted by Sarah Wiggins. 'My, you're looking very well,' she says, 'really got some colour in your cheeks.' And you're left wondering what it is that she's *really* saying. Is she saying that you usually look ill and pale? Is she implying, somehow, that you are melancholic? Does she suspect you're depressed? Christ.

Last night, I was talking to someone who said that they have trouble even *going* into uptight places, which in their case is London. They said that they can't help but take on all that uptightness and tension themselves, and so they prefer just to stay away.

So how can *you* remain free in Uptight Town? Well, I think it can actually be a rather pleasant experience. It serves to remind you how free, relaxed and clear you are when you are suddenly surrounded by people who are uptight, tense and suppressed. If you do feel the uptightness pushing in on you, then simply use it as training. Ask yourself: 'How can I remain conscious and relaxed in this uptight atmosphere?'

> *Ask yourself: 'How can I remain conscious and relaxed in this uptight atmosphere?'*

I actually *like* being around very uptight people sometimes, because it reminds me how well I'm doing. Occasionally I have uptight people bussed into my home – where they storm around being stressed – because it relaxes me so much. They should do that as a service, shouldn't they? (And of course, I have no idea who I mean by 'they'... you know, 'they'; 'thems who sorts things.') They should offer to ship in people who are worse off than you in any difficult situation.

Feeling sick? We'll send in half a dozen people who are more sick, much more sick, than you are. You'll feel better instantly.

Feeling anxious? We'll send you a couple of people who are so anxious that we had to drag them out of their homes in handcuffs to get them here. You'll feel as peaceful as the Dalai Lama when you see these two, believe us.

Feeling uptight and suppressed? We'll send you to England for a long weekend. My, will you feel liberated, relaxed and clear over there in comparison to that lot.

It *is* possible to be free and relaxed and clear in Uptight Town: you say F**k It and embrace it, and you'll most likely feel better yourself when you realize how much more relaxed and clear you are than everyone around you.

SAY F**K IT AND BE SELFISH

We think we have to go to gurus and teachers and priests for wisdom. But every time you fly, one piece of timeless wisdom just passes you by. It occurs during the safety message. I mean, I understand why you're not listening: the brochure full of swanky perfumes and expensive watches is far more interesting than learning how to save your life, isn't it? (No, you're right, though – people just don't survive plane crashes, so you might as well smell nice and have a nice watch to see the time of the moment before you die.)

OK, this is what you're missing: 'In case of a drop in pressure, oxygen masks will drop down from the panel above you. Please be sure to fit your own oxygen mask before attending to the children in your care.'

Bam. It always causes a bit of a shock when I hear this, even before I had children. Of course, if you think about it, it makes eminent sense to sort yourself out quickly and then focus on your children. After all, you're no good to them dead, which is what you could well be once you've struggled trying to get masks on them while you're unable to breathe yourself. But it's still a bit of a shock to receive an official instruction to look after yourself before anyone else – especially your own children.

The backdrop to our slightly shocked response to this message is the following:

* It's good to be selfless.

* It's bad to be selfish.

If you hear on the news that so-and-so carried out a selfless act, then that's something to admire.

If you hear from a girlfriend that so-and-so was just so selfish, then it's never a good thing.

You'd never hear on the news that someone has been lauded for their selfish act. And you'd never hear from your girlfriend that someone was a selfless bastard.

And, like anything that we go through in life without questioning, it's worth having a good look at this one – especially if you're interested in following the way of F**k It.

So just look at your life. Honestly look at what you spend your time doing in the light of whether it is selfish or selfless – or maybe you use other words for now to take away the accustomed meanings of those words: are your actions motivated by self-orientated aims, or with the aim of helping others?

You probably work in order to earn money for yourself (and to give yourself a sense of value, and sometimes to enjoy yourself); you probably spend much of your free time in the pursuit of pleasure for yourself; you go on holiday to satisfy yourself, and so on. Yes, and fair enough, too. That's how most of us live.

If you have a family around you and you want to argue that you're not doing things for yourself but for your family, then I'll ask you: why did you start a family in the first place? Wasn't it for yourself? Don't you gain pleasure from supporting and being with your family? If so, then you're also doing this for yourself.

As normal, 'good' human beings, we are perpetually acting out of self-interest. We are essentially selfish beings. And yet, even as I write that word, there's a charge to it: an implicit:

> *Oh dear, we're not, are we? Well, I'm not, because I always stop for those people on the street who want to sign me up to a life-long direct debit for just what I can afford, which they suggest should be something around £5 a month, which of course doesn't sound much but it all adds up, you know, especially over a lifetime; and it's very difficult for me, you know, to set up a direct debit because my bank prefers me to use the forms they provide, the ones you pick up in the local branch, so, you know, once I just tried to give some real money to the charity, I said: 'Look, I can't do a direct debit just now, but here's £10,' and they said, 'I'm sorry, miss, but we can't take money, we can only do direct debits,' and I thought,* Great, a charity that can't take my money, what's the world coming to? 'Please, miss, I'm starving to death, could you please spare me a direct debit?' *The world's going mad when you can't give money to someone in need...*

So where does this judgement come from? Probably – as usual – from fear. From the fear that if we don't enshrine the concept of selflessness in the heart of our moral code, then we won't give a toss about anyone else – or, more importantly, that no one will give a toss about us when we need it.

But here's the thing: within the whole concept of self-orientated action, of selfishness, is the capacity to help other people. People give money to charity because they feel good about doing so. People help people less fortunate than themselves because it makes them appreciate how lucky they are in their lives. People put themselves out for other people because it gives them a sense of purpose in their lives.

This doesn't reduce the quality of what 'good' people are doing for other people. It just recognizes something in it that most people don't spot.

And it's an important quality to recognize if you ever need to raise money for charity. People are reluctant to just send money off to a cause that will never affect them or their families, and gives no 'return' on their money.

This is why campaigns that allow you to 'adopt an African child' work so well. You get a photograph of the child that you are helping and they write to thank you. This is perfect: you are genuinely helping someone but you're also getting the natural self-orientated satisfaction from doing so.

But here we are again, back in the world of charity. And that takes up only a tiny proportion of our time and money – for most of us, anyway. Let's go back to the family to examine how selfishness versus selflessness works day to day.

When I look at the time I've spent with my family, the only periods I would tag 'selfless' are those when I'm doing things that I don't really want to be doing. If I'm looking after the boys when I'm dog-tired and they're in a state that doesn't suit me at that moment, then I could well tag my persistence in the task 'selfless'.

I certainly do not want to call the majority of my time with my family 'selfless'. If I am working to support my family, I do so because I love it that I'm supporting them. If I'm playing on the beach with my boys, I am doing so for myself as much as for them: that's not selfless.

So it appears – just in my own family situation – that anything that smacks remotely of 'selflessness' is only the times when we're having trouble. Everything else – all the happy, abundant, laughter-filled times – is self-motivated, as we're all getting what we want.

To be selfless is to sacrifice something you want in favour of something that someone else wants (or needs).

In business, it was once the vogue to talk about 'win-win' situations. Win-win is just one (desirable) outcome of several possible outcomes in any negotiation between two parties.

Let's say I run a hot-dog stall and you own a football club. Now, selling hot dogs outside the ground is strictly illegal. And the police

To be selfless is to sacrifice something you want in favour of something that someone else wants (or needs).

have asked you, the owner of the football club, to help stamp it out. So we're talking, face-to-hot-dog-smelling-face.

You tell me your position: you've got to help the police. I tell you my position: this is my living and I sell a lot of hot dogs to fans and they like them. You say you have hot dogs inside the ground. I say people want a hot dog as they're hanging around outside the ground, too, while they're waiting for mates, queuing at the turnstiles. You say that if things carry on as they are, you lose: the police will not get off your back until it's sorted out (i.e., I win, you lose). I say that if you cave in to the police, I lose: I will go out of business. And the fans lose, because they'll lose something that they want (i.e., I lose, you win, but with the unhappy fans, you lose, too, anyway).

So we sit there and think. Look, I say, my hot dogs are good. My stall is clean. I'll get the health and safety to give me a check every week. And maybe you can make me an 'official' hot-dog supplier. OK, you say, that should satisfy the police, that should satisfy the fans, but what about the hot-dog sales I'm losing in the ground? (That was nearly a win-win, but you want your last ounce.)

OK, I say, if I go 'official' I'll raise my prices by 5 per cent and I'll give you the extra. Though it will have to be cash, mind. And you can trust me: I sell hot dogs.

Deal, you say.

And we shake hands. And we have just demonstrated a negotiation to a win-win situation.

In any transaction with the world, it's worth getting to a win-win situation. That's where I am with my family. That's where the charity-giver with the photo of his orphan sitting on his desk is. And it's where you can be in every area of your life.

Why should you sacrifice what you want for what others want or need in:

* your relationship?
* with your family?
* in work?
* with your friends?
* with people less fortunate than yourself?

If you want, you can start to invent new terms for it, like 'enlightened self-interest' or 'proper selfishness'.

In spiritual circles, people talk about 'acting and speaking from their truth'. This is simply like spraying air-freshener over the word 'selfishness' and hoping that no one notices.

So it's worth saying F**k It to selflessness. If you start to feel you're sacrificing yourself in favour of someone else, then you have to get honing your negotiation skills.

Selflessness is a lose-win situation. And they never work out. You end up getting pissed off, and that's no good in the end for the person who seemed to be winning. It's much better if you think you're getting something out of this relationship, too.

The best thing you can do for other people is to put yourself first. Under pressure from the world to be selfless, say F**k It and be selfish.

Selflessness is a lose-win situation.

In the dance of life, pull down your own oxygen mask first, then take a deep breath and help everyone else. They'll thank you for it, believe me.

SAY F**K IT TO YOUR JOB

So, before we get into how shitty working is, let's spend a moment remembering how lucky most of us are today with work.

I can feel the word 'unprecedented' coming up, are you ready? Yes, we live in an age of 'unprecedented' freedom in the workplace. Of course, this doesn't apply to everyone, everywhere, but many of us in the West are experiencing very new freedoms in the workplace. Few areas of work are now restricted to limited groups (i.e., men, people with a posh accent, Oxbridge graduates, etc.). If you're good, if you've got the talent, you can do well in just about whatever you fancy turning your hand to.

Look at how my family has changed, for example. I'll cross family lines as I pick randomly at these examples, but… my great-grandparents were below-stairs staff in a large mansion in the Midlands. My grandparents were working in textile factories, often nights, for the whole of their working lives. My father was offered a choice of two careers by his father: 'You can either work for the gas board or in an accountant's office, lad.' He chose accountancy (which was smart, money-wise).

None of them sat there with a careers 'counsellor' working out how to match their strengths and abilities with a job role. They didn't go to university 'milk-rounds' where they could suck on the teats of 100 corporates. (OK, so all the advisers I ever met tried to ram accountancy and management consultancy down my sore throat, but still…) I was perhaps the first in my family to actually sit there and be able to ask, 'What would I really like to do?' The answer was something creative, so that's what I did.

Of course, things can still be difficult. But if you decide that you don't want to land in the local call-centre (or whatever jobs are most available down the road from where you live now), then there are unprecedented opportunities to get the hell out of there and make a success of something else.

And yet … and yet … all this freedom, all this opportunity, all this wealth and most of us are still not happy. Many of us don't like the work we do or the company we're working for. Work is what we spend most of our time doing, yet many of us are fundamentally unhappy with what we get up to between the hours of 9 a.m. and 7 p.m. There is always trouble at the mill.

The first reason is that there's usually too much expectation. The workplace is as littered with unrealistic expectations as it is with crass clichés. Just think about the expectations that surround you and the job that you do: from parents, from friends, from society, from your employer, from your staff, from shareholders, from the government. We do what we do because we think it should be fulfilling us, that there's the possibility of attaining all those material needs (and aims) we have. We expect a lot from a job. Your workplace is now probably also the most important community you belong to.

Many of us are fundamentally unhappy with our work.

So your job has a lot to hold in terms of expectations. And the problem is that many of these may be competing with each other: your parents want something to brag about at dinner parties; your partner wants a fat pay cheque; your boss wants long hours and high productivity; and you want to spend more time sitting in the park, reading.

It's time to unpick the expectations. Work out what other people are expecting of you (and whether it really matters to you), work out what you are expecting of yourself (and whether that really matters to you). Start to say F**k It to the things that you find actually don't matter so much. Concentrate on the few things that *do* matter to you and make you feel good. I saw a great comedian last week in London: he was a trained GP (not, I suspect, and hope, that there are many untrained GPs), had said F**k It and started doing stand-up comedy.

Given we're talking about business, I'll employ my own cliché again: you can't please all of the people all of the time. So don't try. Start trying to please yourself more and see what happens.

Which brings us to the second reason: too little expectation. If you can relax enough to really feel what you fancy doing, and what you really can't bear doing, then it's worth setting up some expectations about sorting yourself out. If you can't bear the job you're in, expect that you're going to find something better within a month. Expecting positive change (especially when you know specifically what that change should be) works.

And don't get into too much stress about making decisions, moving on, etc. When you really know what you want (through relaxing), it's very difficult for change not to happen quite naturally. It may be that the day after you've realized you'd be mad to carry on working where you are, you get a call from someone who knows of a job elsewhere. Once you're free from the expectations of you, just start to rest in your own expectations for yourself.

Saying F**k It in the context of work isn't just about giving up your job, though. It could be that as you relax, you realize you're actually content with the work you do. You may find that simply accepting what you have is the best way to say F**k It. You may find that any unhappiness you feel is from others' (or your own) unrealistic expectations of yourself. Are you going for the director's job because you want it or because you think that's what you *should* be doing? Do you really need to jump to the next level up and work harder, or could you make do with what you have and maybe even work less?

In my experience, one of the most common statements people make about work is: 'Well, I don't really know what I want to do yet.' I hear this from people in their 30s and 40s, not just those in their 20s. People go on saying this for years and years. And this is the only articulation they have for a deep sense of things not being right. They've chosen their work area to articulate this unease, but the reasons for the unease are probably more complex. What they're really saying is, 'I don't know myself, but I get the feeling there's something wrong in there.'

If this is speaking to you, it's time to stop hiding behind the words 'I don't really know what I want to do yet.' Say F**k It and find the courage to get to know yourself. What do you really want of yourself and for yourself? Find somebody who can help you work it through if you fancy, but the chances are it's not just about your job, it's about your life. And I guess the problem for you is what most of us face: that we have many competing (usually unknown) forces at work in us.

> *Say F**k It and find the courage to get to know yourself.*

I noticed this phenomenon on my last trip to the UK: everybody wants to be 'everything'. There's so much pressure on people to be everything that it's irresistible. We all want to be successful at work, experts in the home (at cooking, gardening, DIY), hard-working employees, present and available partners and parents, home-owners and wealthy.

We all want to live sustainable lifestyles, be on-the-ball mentally and culturally, feel relaxed and peaceful, see the world, but not fly too often. Everything's speeding up in a performance culture. Even in yoga classes, people are looking around wondering how quickly they'll be able to do that difficult-looking *asana*, or whether the *pranayama* exercise can bring peace to every area of their life.

I feel tense just writing about it.

Of course, sifting through your own desires is difficult. You'd like to be financially secure – with a home abroad – but also to work less in a less stressful job. Some desires can sit next to each other, while some compete. Start working it out.

Me? I don't usually do any work. I just do things I like. And I've stopped liking writing about work, so it's time to move on.

SAY F**K IT TO YOUR COUNTRY

In the original edition of this book, I observed that most Britons were moving to France and most Poles were moving to Britain. All over the world people were – and still are – saying F**k It and changing country. For me, it would be much easier if we could just do a Country Swap, just as they do with houses.

We could swap for 10 years then swap back again. It would, after all, have been neater if Poland could offer some rambling, rustic homes (like France), near the sea (like Spain), with Italian food (like Italy), so that all those Brits tired of the rat race could simply have swapped homes with all those Poles, who want nothing better than to work hard and get the chance to make a fortune and spend it on lots of stuff made by other people making a fortune.

The truth is that after 10 years (sometimes less, sometimes more), the Brits will want some action (culture, wealth and something awful to moan about) and the Poles will be sick to death of the rat race and fancy some country house, lying in the sun, eating Italian food.

I swapped countries. I now live in a warmer, more relaxed, more laid-back, happier, less competitive country (Italy), and I'm happy with that. When I go back to the UK I find it – in about equal measures – inspiring, motivating, alive, buzzing… but also overcrowded, over-competitive, striving, messy, uptight and neurotic.

It's another expression of modern freedom that many of us have the ability to move to a different country without having been forced out of our own (through war, starvation, etc.).

If you've had enough, and you want more sun, why not? Say F**k It and get on a plane (or, more responsibly, on a train – or, even more responsibly, walk it). But here's something to remember first: we take ourselves with us wherever we go.

Here's something to remember first: we take ourselves with us wherever we go.

This is, of course, obvious. In a very literal way, we can't help but take ourselves with us. We don't have a to do list saying 'passport, tickets, skeleton, internal organs, musculature and all the bits in between'. But we do tend to take with us all the problems that we assume were caused by things around us. If you think you're unhappy because of the rain, the people, your job, the uptight men – whatever it is you think you're running away from – have another think. Because the chances are that all the unhappiness is within you.

And wherever you go – whatever paradise you find – all that unhappiness will come bubbling back up again sooner or later. Now, of course, it may take giving it all up and living somewhere else to really realize this. Even though I'm telling you this right now, you probably don't believe it – in which case it's best to get on with it so you can prove to yourself that this is the truth, and then get on with your life.

I do know this through experience. I helped three burly men pack up a lorry with our stuff. I thought I was keeping my eye on the stuff: making sure they didn't break anything precious, or leave bits behind that we wanted, or pick up things that we didn't want. But somehow, somewhere in that lorry were hidden all my issues, anxieties, anger, annoying habits and irrational mood swings.

So, I'm here now, sitting in what you would probably think is a paradise, with a lot of the same shit going on. Though for me, the very process of realizing that I am all that stuff wherever I go has been very liberating. And I may not have got to that liberation if I'd stayed sitting at that desk in London.

Relax, let go and then see if you really need to move. If you prefer to stay, then accept your life and your country for what it is. The worst thing is not to act and to spend the rest of your life in Blighty moaning about it.

SAY F**K IT TO SEARCHING

We're all searchers. We're always looking for more meaning. The search is relatively unconscious for much of our life. We search for meaning in relationships, in friendships, in jobs, in money, in hobbies, in 'missions' to help other people.

> *We're all searchers. We're always looking for more meaning.*

We're very lucky in Western society because many people have unparalleled opportunities to get what they want. There is more freedom of work, of movement, of belief, of sexuality than there has ever been.

So, in your search for meaning and satisfaction, you can get to the place you're after relatively quickly. For those who think that true meaning and satisfaction lie in getting their dream job, or finding their dream lover, or owning a BMW, if they really put their mind to it, they can actually achieve it.

What tends to happen, though, is once the object is achieved or owned, we then move on to the next thing. And the next, and the next.

If this happens often enough, people get to the point where they think to themselves, *There must be more to life than this*. And they tend to get spiritual. This is great. This is why it's a blessing to be rich and successful — it means you get to the point of realizing riches and success don't mean a lot more quickly than those who don't have them.

This, of course, doesn't mean that only rich and successful people have the wisdom to get spiritual. It's just one example of an area of search. If you think that meaning and satisfaction reside in the pursuit and finding of love, then it's a blessing if you get to shag enough people or have enough 'meaningful' relationships to realize that 'there must be more to life than this'.

If you think that meaning and satisfaction reside in your spotting every train in the UK, one by one (i.e., trainspotting), then it's a blessing if you get to spot them all as quickly as possible so you too can get to realize that 'there must be more to life than this'.

For whatever reason, people get spiritual apparently towards the end of their pursuit of meaning.

And nowadays, 'spiritual' means a whole supermarket of possible goods and services. Previously in the UK, there was just a corner shop at the end of your street that sold the same thing to everyone: Spam. And Christianity was the Spam of the past. Sure, you could add Spam to other things to get a slightly different twist: Spam with chips, Spam with eggs, Spam in mashed potato, even Spam with Spam. Just as there are Protestants and Catholics and Jehovah's Witnesses. But they are all still Spam with a twist.

Nowadays shopping is a huge out-of-town affair with every possible food catering to all possible tastes – ethnic, ready-meal, frozen, etc. And similarly, we can choose from all the different organized religions – Christianity, Islam, Hinduism – or the ones that look like religions – Buddhism – or the ones that are structured, but nothing like religions: yoga, shamanism, Taoism.

What many people tend to do, of course, is go to the pick 'n' mix counter. They take a scoopful of yoga, add a bit of Buddhism, have a little taste of Taoism, a sprinkle of the latest wisdom vogue, a bit of *The Power of Now*, some new-age philosophies about abundance and karma and so on.

Of course, they don't buy any meat, and sometimes no dairy produce, and often bypass the bread, too (there I go a-mixing the metaphors again), but off they go to the checkout with a whole basket-full of stuff.

And now supermarkets sell things they never used to: clothes, books, DVDs. And this is the world of alternative therapy. From a regular massage to Chinese medicine and Reiki and homoeopathy – these extras all have a spiritual edge that becomes part of your new belief system, even if it's as basic as, 'I believe massage helps to calm me down.'

In the olden days, if you went to the corner shop and bought a tin of Spam and some potatoes, there was a good chance the next person would buy the same thing. That's how belief and religion were, too: we were all doing practically the same thing.

Today, if you look at the baskets and trolleys going through the checkouts, you'll see that no two are the same. They're packed full of a huge variety of goods. And for most of us, that's how it is with our belief systems, too: they're different from each other, and relatively complicated.

But at one very basic level, nothing has changed: belief and spirituality are very meaningful. And, to many people, they're everything.

And as we already know, meaning creates tension and pain when it comes into conflict with what life is. So the more meaningful your belief/spirituality/religion is, the more potential for tension and pain:

* If you believe it's wrong to be gay, then gay people will make you tense and judgemental.

* If you believe it's wrong to have sex before marriage, then every moment of lust and desire will drive you mad.

* If you believe in abundance, then giving away your money and not getting 10 times in return will piss you off.

* If you believe in the power of peace over all, then wars will upset you.

* If you believe that the meek shall inherit the Earth, then it makes you angry to see the powerful and rich having a good time in the meantime.

* If you believe a woman should cover herself up from head to toe, then any revealed female flesh will make you angry.

* If you believe that God will have His day, then you don't appreciate this day as much.

* If you believe the powers of evil should be crushed, you might commit acts of 'evil' to achieve this.

* If you believe the answer lies in the afterlife, you miss the answers in this life.

* If you believe in past lives, you can give up responsibility for your present one.

* If you believe that Jesus will return to save you, you forget that there's nothing to save you from.

* If you believe that non-judgement is the way to peace, your own judgement causes you pain and guilt.

So here's another cosmic joke: the search in our lives leads us to try to find meaning beyond what 'is' in our lives. Our loves, our money, our achievements are not quite enough, so we look for more. And we look for it in 'spirituality', which usually involves the 'unseen'.

The answer to everything possibly lies in this: not looking for more meaning, but looking for less.

Whereas the answer to everything possibly lies in this: not looking for more meaning, but looking for less.

When we strip away meaning from the things that are already meaningful in our lives, that's where we find peace and the divine.

This is the joke:

God is not more than we know. He's less than we know.

The less you search, the more you find.

The less you want, the more you receive.

The less you look, the more you see.

The less 'You', the more 'Is'.

If God is less when we're looking for more, then spirituality is not some preserve of believers. Spirituality is everything as it is.

Everyone is spiritual, as is everything. And everything you do is spiritual and divine:

If you're upset and angry, that's spiritual.

If you're jealous, that's spiritual.

If you're hungry, that's spiritual.

If you want to own a Porsche, that's spiritual.

If you want to strangle your boss, that's spiritual.

Nothing is *not* spiritual.

This means that there's nothing you have to do to be spiritual or 'good'. You don't have to go anywhere or achieve anything. You can truly say F**k It to the whole thing and still be spiritual.

Because it is impossible *not* to be spiritual.

SAY F**K IT, AND LIVE AND LET LIVE

I like tea. Gaia likes tea. We both like tea. And, which is fortunate for a married couple, we like the same kind of tea – Rooibos, which we have with soya milk and honey. Isn't that a lovely thing to share? Not only our love of that particular tea, but the precise way in which we 'take' it.

Well, I say precise, but it's not quite that, because Gaia likes a little more honey than I do. Well, I say a little, I've calculated that she likes 50 per cent more honey than I do, because I like one teaspoonful of honey and she likes more.

The thing is, she prefers to use a larger spoon – a dessert spoon – for serving and stirring the aforementioned honey into the aforementioned tea. She doesn't use a teaspoon and serve one and a half measures, as I would do if I preferred to take my tea with a little more honey. She likes to go for the less precise measure of a dessert spoon that's *around* 75 per cent full.

I see her making her tea (and sometimes mine) and it annoys me. Why would she choose a spoon so *not* designed for the job in hand when there is another spoon that does it perfectly? It's called a TEAspoon, and it sits in the compartment next to her spoon in the cutlery drawer.

Now, I know what you're thinking: actually, that's quite logical, because her serving preference is MORE THAN one teaspoon, it makes sense to use a larger spoon. After all, it's more efficient (there's only one journey from honey jar to tea cup), and it's better for the honey jar in the end, as Gaia is not returning to the jar with a spoon that's just been dipped in a cup of tea.

But Gaia is not doing this for a logical reason. No. I know that.

Oh, and one more thing: it's much harder to stir a cup of tea with a dessert spoon than it is with a teaspoon Much harder.

So I tell her how silly it is to use a dessert spoon rather than a teaspoon:

'Look love, it's not just that, in my humble opinion, the smaller spoon is better for the job, both in measuring and in stirring, these serving implements are blessed with something relatively rare in the kitchen.'

'What's that, John? What are they blessed with, pray tell?'

'They're blessed with names that indicate their ideal purpose... one called 'tea' and the other called 'dessert'. So why on earth would you want to use a dessert spoon for tea?'

'I just like it. It suits me. It's the spoon for me. And it's none of your business.'

Well, it is actually. Because you, Gaia, use your bloody dessert spoon to serve honey in *my* tea, and the measure is therefore all over the bloody place. Sometimes, it's far too much (if you're not thinking and give me a 'Gaia serving'), and sometimes it's far too little (if you're giving me what you think I'd like, but are unable to judge because YOU'RE USING THE WRONG BLOODY SPOON).

Gaia likes to use this spoon because it also demonstrates her freedom – her ability to choose to live her life in the way that she wants. Sure, it's wonderful that we have so much in common, she's saying, but I'M NOT YOU, and I'M NOT YOURS, and I will demonstrate my freedom, my separateness. I will remind you that I can live my own life, by making my own idiosyncratic, illogical spoon choice.

And of course, for a peaceful life, I must live and let live. I must 'tea' while she 'desserts', even if we're both drinking tea. When I don't mention the presence of the outsized spoon in the teacup, Gaia feels respected and appreciated; she feels as if she's being given space in the relationship.

> *For a peaceful life, I must live and let live.*

When I'm in a grumpy mood and I do mention it, she feels suffocated. So I try to work with it. One day, in some crazy moment of spoonular generosity, I tried to use a dessert spoon myself for the tea. But it was a disaster. I wildly overhoneyed and the resulting 'honey-rush' made me emotional. I lifted the oversized spoon out of the tea and gazed at my inverted reflection, seeing myself a little teary. So it was back to the teaspoon for me. That's me living. And the dessert spoon is Gaia living.

That's live and let live for you.

4

THE
EFFECT
OF
SAYING
F**K IT

LIFE RESPONDS WHEN YOU SAY F**K IT TO IT

You've taken your two kids out for a Chinese meal. Flynn is five and Lizzie is seven. You are tired. The crispy duck is taking a while to arrive and the kids are getting restless. Flynn unfolds the starched serviette, puts it on his head and starts making 'Ooohhhh, oooohhh' noises, as if he's a ghost. Lizzie joins in before you've had a chance to utter a word.

The 'oohhhhhhs' rapidly rise in volume and you ask the kids to stop it: 'We're in a restaurant and you'll disturb other people.' In fact, those other people are already starting to get disturbed and are looking round.

Your initial pleas have no effect, and you now have several courses of action open to you:

* You get heavy and use whatever methods you normally employ to control your children (these could range from bribery, such as 'You won't get an ice cream', to the creation of fear, such as 'You wait until I get you home' or 'I'll tell your dad about this').

* You don't get heavy at all, but get increasingly frustrated that your kids are not listening to you – this usually ends in some outburst on your part.

* You give in and just go with it.

No. 1 works if your methods are good enough, or if you are scary enough. Well, it may work on this occasion. But kids are kids, and unless you make them very, very scared of you, they will constantly resist your attempts to control them.

No. 2 involves no serious attempt to control your kids, but no acceptance of them either. This is a hopeless place to be in and is the cause of the most stress.

No. 3 is the hardest and riskiest to do because it goes against everything that parents are told about discipline and boundaries.

But imagine this: you put your own serviette on your head and start 'ooohhhing', too. The kids love it and 'oohhh' back for a while. But you know what happens? They soon get bored and move on to something else that is – usually – quieter and less disturbing to other people. And those other people soon forget that they've been disturbed in the first place.

Child-rearing discourses aside, let's look at a child as a metaphor for life.

Most of us – as we have discussed – try to control our lives to the smallest detail. We have very sophisticated methods for controlling life, in fact, just like the parent who used method No. 1.

You might well see some of these methods in action in your parents. Parents are past masters at the trying-to-control-life game. Parents – usually with the aid of more monetary resources than they had when they were younger – try to eliminate all forms of discomfort from their lives.

They set up comfortable routines, fill their houses with comforting ornaments, and rugs to put on toilet seats, and talk about things that threaten no one, such as the best route to Cirencester or how to put up sheds. They eat comforting foods (creamy things, baked things, roasted things) and watch comforting television (like shows about baking).

But as their methods get more and more sophisticated/desperate, life seems to bugger around with their plans to an even greater extent. The house gets broken into, pipes burst, they get ill and people start dying all over the place.

The controlled and 'comfortable' life is not the path of wisdom or happiness, I'm afraid. But neither is the half-baked attempt to control life with method No. 2.

No. 2 is a shit way to live. At least the controller has some vim, some direction. When you are trying to control but not quite sure, you are just knocked around on the stormy sea of life. You're pissed off, but can't quite be bothered enough to get up to do something about it.

This is the path to misery.

When we give in to life – when we say F**k It at any level – we begin to ride on the wave of life. When you stick the serviette on your own head, a few things happen:

* You actually enjoy yourself, because the game is a good one and you've stopped resisting it.

* The kids love you for it and may even remember this for the rest of their lives – without the normal parental resistance to what they're doing, they usually stop what they're doing much sooner than you'd expect.

So, I'm sorry to be shoving you in and out of metaphors, especially when they're close to home… but the same thing happens with life. When you give in to life, the same things happen:

* You start enjoying yourself, because the game of life is a good one and you've stopped resisting it.

* Life seems to love it when you stop resisting and starts coming your way more.

* Life ebbs and flows very naturally of its own accord. If you hit something nasty, it's soon replaced naturally by something lovely.

Of course, the second statement is the one that you might be wondering about the most. This is counter-intuitive. We are taught that, to get anything in life, we have to work hard and strive for it. We have to set goals and work towards them. We have to work out what matters to us and ruthlessly put those things first and try to nurture them. We believe that if we don't really strive for things, then we won't get them. But, possibly, the opposite is true.

If we find the courage to loosen our hold on things… to stop wanting things so much… to stop working so hard and striving so much… to give up some of the things that matter to us… something magical happens:

We naturally start getting what we originally wanted,
but without the effort.

Now this is very zen and potentially very confusing: to get what you want you must give up wanting it.

But look at it like this: any form of desire and striving involves some form of tension. When you let go of the desire, the tension goes. And the relaxation that replaces it tends to attract good things into your life.

Back to the child metaphor: when you give up wanting so much for your children – wanting them to be top of the class, the best at sport, go to the best university and get the best job – when you truly give these desires up and you just sit back and let your children be, they feel absolute freedom.

*Say F**k It and life will be so grateful it will shower you with blessings.*

And, funnily enough, in their sense of freedom they tend to excel in whatever they turn their attention to. So you get what you wanted, precisely through *not* wanting it.

When you give up wanting everything to be just so – when you say F**k It – life will be so grateful it will shower you with blessings.

THE EFFECT ON YOUR MIND OF SAYING F**K IT

You notice the beauty in unexpected things

Have you ever watched a young child playing? Or can you remember what was going on inside your head as a child? I've done both – the first when my boys were young, and the second when I really relax, because I remember then what it was like to be a child.

If I lie down and look up into a blue sky and listen to the sound of a distant aeroplane, it invariably brings up a memory from my childhood. Why? Because as we grow up, we stop being fascinated by ordinary things. So when I do occasionally take pleasure simply in what's around me, it reminds me of the last time I did that: when I was a child.

Children live in the miracle of existence.

This is what children do. They live in the miracle of existence. Everything is new and fascinating. They can enjoy the wrapping as much as the present… a leaking tap as much as a beautiful lake… the smell of rain falling on dry concrete as much as the smell of baking bread.

There are no rules about what's good or bad, what's better than something else, or what's worth it. There's little discernment: there are just things coming in… and most of them are fascinating.

As we grow up, we learn how to discern, discriminate and filter out. And we tend to filter out the ordinary things in favour of the extraordinary and the unusual. In fact, much of the time we're so lost in thoughts of the past or worries about the future that we don't have much time for any kind of appreciation. But when we do, it tends to be the things that adults think are worth appreciating: tasty things, beautiful things, interesting things and expensive things.

At some point the feeling of wooden boards under our feet, the sound of a toilet flushing in a room upstairs, the feeling of wind against our face… these all disappear off the list of things that we should appreciate. Instead we spend lots of money to go on holiday, or go to the theatre or go out for a meal in order to flex our appreciation muscles.

When we say F**k It to anything, the meanings start to crumble as the things that matter lose their meaning, and then suddenly the world opens up again. Without the discrimination and discernment we learned as we were growing up, every single thing has the potential to be appreciated. Everything is beautiful.

If this happens all of a sudden, it can be mind-blowing (almost literally). And this is what happens to a lot of people who have apparently 'awakened'. When you start seeing the beauty in absurd things, you know you are starting to lose your mind. Or at least the mind that has learned to see meaning in only a limited range of things.

See each moment as having infinite potential for beauty.

See each moment as having infinite potential for beauty. We tend to drag all our judgements, conditioning and boundaries from the past into the present. And it squashes that moment into something very limited. If you leave some of those judgements behind and just see things as young children might see them, you start to get a beautiful feeling. It's a feeling of relief but mixed with some kind of longing, too. The longing rises up from a very deep part of you that remembers what it was like to see things like this all the time.

When we say F**k It, we turn the clock back. We unlearn meaning and smash the things that we have come to think matter. We regress to a more natural state where things don't mean much but they're all just so bloody beautiful.

Anxiety evaporates over time

When anything that matters goes pear-shaped, you feel anxious and stressed. In fact, simply the possibility of the things that matter going pear-shaped makes you feel anxious and stressed.

Given the vast range of things that matter to us, there's a hell of a lot of potential for anxiety. And anxiety and stress will make you ill over time. So it's worth trying to give them up and using the patches instead.

> When you begin to say F**k It to things, the anxiety vanishes.

When you begin to say F**k It to things, the anxiety vanishes. Late for work and stressed about it? Say F**k It and the stress disappears immediately.

The more you say F**k It, the more you'll realize that most things don't matter that much really. And your anxiety, over time, will evaporate.

Sure, you'll still get anxious around some things, but that's life. And anxiety in the right context can be a useful response. If you're driving your car down a country road and you round a corner to find an elephant hurtling towards you, it's helpful to feel a tad anxious. Your adrenaline will start to pump, giving you all sorts of special powers that will help you deal effectively with the imminent threat.

If the adrenaline is not enough, and the only scenario is a good squashing by said elephant, then, by all means, say F**k It before you go.

It may make your ride to heaven a little easier. This is, of course, belief-dependent, as the very use of the word 'Fuck' might send you to hell in some belief systems.

Your views change and become less rigid

I've always felt a little sorry for politicians. Well, someone has to, don't they? They have to work out what they believe on every issue under the sun – which is hard enough in itself – and they then have to stick to it for the rest of their lives.

There's room for a tiny bit of manoeuvre, of course, over a whole political lifetime. But very little. And rethinking is slammed as a 'U-turn'.

Now, as long as I'm not putting other cars at risk, I'm all in favour of the U-turn. If you realize you've been going the wrong way, it's much better to slam on the brakes and screech round onto the other carriageway, like they do in American movies.

You never hear politicians say: 'Look, I've actually sat down and thought about this properly, and I realize I've been a complete arse. I now think precisely the opposite to before. Sorry.'

Along with our relentless accumulation of meaning, we accumulate views on everything. And these tend to become more fixed as we get older. Of course, views come in every shape and size, but they're still views.

You may have views on big subjects: that no one should be allowed to starve, that persecution should not be tolerated, that nuclear powers should be disarmed. You may have views on small subjects: that Sue down the road should kick out Mick after that fling he had with Mandy, that the chip shop on the corner should bring back the battered Mars bars, that the new weather girl on the local news channel shouldn't wear such short skirts.

But they're all still views. And all views are related to something that matters. When you start to say F**k It and things begin to matter less, then you start to lose your love of views. Ultimately, if nothing mattered at all, then you'd have no views at all. You'd have no position, no stance, no argument. You'd just react to things as they happened: completely freshly.

In the process of things mattering less, your views may change. They'll certainly become less rigid.

People who start to say F**k It turn from vegetarians to meat-eaters, from activists in a cause to passivists, from pacifists to apathists. And if I've made up a few words there for the sake of a point and a rhythm, hey, F**k It.

I once held the view that English should be written correctly. That you shouldn't start a sentence with 'and' or 'but', for example. But one day I said F**k It. And now I'm starting every other sentence with such conjunctions, I'm using fucking fuck every other word, and I'm making up newly fancivist words.

These days, my only real view is out of my eyes, in this moment.

I once had a prepared view on everything. This is a sad confession, but when politicians were asked questions on the radio or telly, I'd imagine how I'd answer. These days, my only real view is out of my eyes, in this moment.

You lose the plot

No, I don't mean you'll go potty. Although of course you might – and even if you don't, it may appear to people around you that you have. This is what I mean by losing the plot:

Let's say your life is a film. The 'plot' of your life is something you have pretty well figured out at the moment (well, you think so anyway):

* You have a good idea about how the main character (i.e., you) will act in given circumstances.

* You know what's gone before and you pretty much understand it.

* You recognize, and understand, the setting of each scene.

* You have pretty good ideas about what should happen in the rest of the play/film.

* You have a very clear sense of a beginning, a middle and an end.

When you start to say F**k It to things, everything softens and blurs. The film suddenly starts to look more like a French movie from the 1960s. Your French has gone, though, so you can't understand the dialogue, and the subtitles are slightly too small from where you're sitting.

More specifically, this is what happens:

* Given the rules that the main character (i.e., you) acts by are crumbling, it gets less and less easy to see what he or she will do in any given circumstance.

* The meaning of what has happened to you becomes less clear and your past somehow seems less solid.

* The setting of each scene suddenly becomes vast and full of possibilities, whereas before you were only seeing what you wanted to see.

* You plan less and less; you may lose a sense of purpose and you see that your life could go in any (infinite) number of directions.

* Your perception of time shifts and you realize that there is only really a middle: a present moment of existence.

THE EFFECT ON YOUR BODY OF SAYING F**K IT

The body softens

If we have a tense thought, then that tension is also represented in the body. So if you release a tense thought by saying F**k It, you begin to release the tension in your body.

Just have a go with one thing now. Pick something that you're anxious about today. You probably don't have to look very far. Take a big inbreath and think about that thing and how anxious it makes you feel. Then, as you breathe out, say F**k It and feel the release in your body. Do this again.

If this can happen with one thing in your life, imagine what would happen if you could do it to a whole range of things. When you really start to say F**k It in your life, your whole body will begin to soften. You may not notice it at first, but it will certainly start to happen. In fact, other people might notice it before you do. Your face will soften, so people may remark that you look younger. Your neck and shoulders will soften, so you may stop having those headaches, or aches and pains in those areas. All your muscles will soften and feel heavier.

As your body softens, you will catch yourself just sitting and enjoying the feelings in your body. And one of those feelings will be *chi*.

Your *chi* flows

The more you say F**k It and the more you relax, the more your *chi* will flow.

Chi, remember, is the life-force that flows through you. You will feel it as a tingling or a warmth or a magnetic feeling.

If you don't know what it feels like, it's time to learn how to play the energy accordion. So don your energetic beret, eat some energy garlic and pick up an imaginary accordion.

Now, this accordion really enjoys being played slowly – very slowly. So your hands are apart, holding the accordion. And now you start to bring your hands closer together. Don't let them touch. Just bring them slowly together. When they are very close together, start to pull the accordion open again. And continue this process. Close your eyes and focus on what you're feeling in and between your hands.

The more you relax, the more you can feel.

The main thing here is to relax. Relax your shoulders, relax your hands. If you don't get it today, give it a rest; you'll get it tomorrow.

But what you begin to feel, today or tomorrow, is *chi*.

And this stuff is the key to your health.

I love working with *chi* because it has the simplest principle: the more you relax, the more you can feel. It's not necessary to learn complicated techniques, or go from beginner classes to intermediate, then advanced, classes. No, just know that the more you relax, the more you'll feel.

So when you say F**k It to anything, because you're releasing tension in the body, more *chi* will be flowing.

Your body will rebalance itself

Any tension in the body creates an energy imbalance.

In Chinese medicine, all the meridians that flow around the body are related to different energetic organ systems. If you create physical tension in any of these areas, you create a block to the energy flow that has an effect on that organ system.

Imagine how you are at work. You may well be hunched over a computer all day, worrying about this or that. The hunching alone creates tension in your shoulders, neck and back, and the worried thoughts on top of this simply add to the tension. And you can sit like that for hours.

All that tension is blocking the vital flow of energy around the body, and you begin to get imbalances. An energetic imbalance will start to affect how you are – your emotions and feelings – and it will also begin to affect your health.

Whenever you say F**k It and relax into something you were previously tense around, the energy will begin to flow through what was previously blocked. Your energy system will begin to rebalance itself.

Illnesses will disappear

Given that illnesses are created by these energy imbalances, any rebalancing will lead to the releasing of illness.

This is what happens when you have acupuncture. The needles are placed in points where energy blocks are occurring and – wham bam – the energy starts to flow again.

If you relax enough, you get exactly the same effect.

Every time you say F**k It to something, it can be like one well-placed needle in your body. So you will begin to feel better. You will feel like you have more energy (and we're talking about the traditional stuff this time, not *chi* energy). You may need less sleep and less food. And illnesses will begin to subside and heal.

You will live longer

The effect of all this relaxing is, ultimately, to increase the length of your life. (Horrible life-shortening accidents aside, of course.)

If you say F**k It to one big area of tension in your life, you are going to increase the amount of time you spend on this Earth. Whenever you relax fully, you slow down the process of ageing. If you can relax really deeply, you can reverse the process of ageing.

So, funnily enough, the less life means to you, the more of it you get.

THE EFFECT ON YOUR SPIRIT OF SAYING F**K IT

This section was written before any of the other words in this book – more than a year earlier, actually. It was part of another book I was working on, one with a different title.

While I was writing the first draft of F**k It: The Ultimate Spiritual Way, I added a lot of material from that earlier book at that point, and changed the introduction so it was relevant (mainly by adding the words 'F**k It'!).

The text that follows is actually much reduced from what I found in my files, but it is the roots of F**k It. When I re-read it recently, I realized that, at the time, I must have concluded that it wasn't right for the original book. When you read it, I think you'll see why: the philosophy it outlines is uncompromising stuff. But, in fact, it's because this philosophy is so uncompromising and difficult that the whole F**k It thing was conceived in the first place, so I decided to include it in this new edition. I wanted you to see some of where this all came from.

It's headache time

For years, Gaia and I had been interested in the (largely Eastern) idea of 'oneness': the perception that we are all one. The idea of oneness isn't new, and you'll find it popping up in most philosophies and religions (usually on the fringes). We were particularly interested in the teachings of 'Advaita', which means 'not two' (i.e., one – durr!); it's also referred to as 'non-dualism' (i.e., oneism – durr!).

If you ever get the chance to go to a talk (or 'satsang') by an Advaita teacher, don't miss it. It will be fascinating. And it will give you a headache. In fact, these talks should be sponsored by a headache-relieving painkiller like Anadin, because, despite the fact that the philosophy of 'oneness' resonates very strongly with many of us (i.e., its truth is deeply understood), our brains struggle to comprehend it.

But how else *could* it be? An individual's individual brain will always have trouble with the idea that individuality is just a part of the 'dream' of oneness – and that *there is no individual*. (OK, OK, go get the Hedex… you see there how I just advertised, in the name of balance, another brand of painkiller?)

*Our discovery of 'F**k It' suddenly made everything work for me.*

So, back then, I was feeling the notion of everything being one; I was getting it, but I was also struggling with it, as the 'I' does. But I couldn't escape that sense of freedom I was sniffing.

Then, our discovery of 'F**k It' suddenly made everything work for me. Saying F**k It was pointing to, and seemed to be arising from, this alternate perception of reality. By saying it, I felt that freedom. I realized that the 10,000 things of my everyday, apparently individual and separated existence didn't matter so much (if at all).

Saying 'F**k It' allowed me to keep in touch with that alternate view of reality, without struggling when I wasn't getting it.

Let me explain what I mean by this. When I make music, I use a piece of software called Ableton Live. With this, I can work with what I create in two different 'views'. One is a linear time track, where I can see the music developing over time – a bit like reading sheet music – and the other is a clip-based view, where I see the samples that are currently running, and those that could be initiated.

To switch between these two views, I hit the 'tab' key. What I see in each view looks very different. In fact, it appears to be the *opposite* of the other (one is a time-based view of the music; the other is a moment-by-moment snapshot of the unfolding music). But underneath both views is the same thing: the same sounds, samples, and instruments, and the same code). Both opposite views are true, at the same time.

Most of us 'view' reality in one way: we see solid, individual shapes interacting with one another in a Newtonian world. But sometimes we inadvertently hit 'tab' and the view changes – we see that all is one, all is connected, all is potential, all is vibrating energy, all is God, etc. I use this metaphor to understand my own relationship with reality. These are opposite views of reality, but to me, both appear to be true. I don't live in one paradigm denying the existence of the other. I don't live in one paradigm longing to be in the other.

'F**k It' has become my tab key.

As I was writing the original edition of this book, I became very excited about the idea of saying to people: 'Look, there's a tab key here that gives you another view of reality, and that view is refreshing and liberating. You don't have to keep your finger on the key – you don't have to see that view all the time – but try hitting that button occasionally and see how you feel.'

I was also excited about offering what I felt were profound insights in a simple and accessible way. And if anyone ever says, 'Well, it's a bit too simple, isn't it?', I can now send them to this section to see where it all came from. Sure, I'm still trying to convey the ideas in an accessible way, but the ideas are not easy.

So, let's go. You'll see that I mention 'F**k It' in the first few paragraphs, as I attempted to make the (earlier) text relevant, but that then drops away as you read the pure original text.

Fasten your seat belts, and enjoy the ride.

Things matter less, if at all

You're walking in the countryside on a summer's day. You decide to strike out from the footpath and make your own course across the hills. In so doing you won't immediately make another footpath. No, of course not. However, if you follow your tracks perfectly on your return from your destination, and then make the same journey the following day, and the day after that, and so on, you will eventually make a new footpath.

It's a beautiful state to be in when things don't matter so much.

And that's what happens when we say F**k It to more and more things in our lives. Our brains start to get used to the paradigm shift from things mattering to things not mattering. And after a while, we might really begin to see that things don't really matter at all.

It becomes an instinct. When things are stressing us out (because they matter too much), we just say F**k It.

It's a beautiful state to be in when things don't matter so much. And it doesn't mean you'll go round like a sulky teenager saying 'don't care' or 'can't be bothered'. When the tension is lost around the things that matter, everything around you just becomes beautiful for what it is.

Of course, the great spiritual truth of this whole caboodle is that *absolutely nothing matters*. Nothing matters at all. Not in the slightest.

You give up seeking.

Your life has been like a long, hard day at work. You thought it would never end. You were looking at the clock so often by the end of the day that you could have sworn it had stopped.

And now you're home. You've had your plate of spaghetti bolognese in front of your favourite soap. You've poured yourself a glass of wine. You've kicked off your shoes and put your feet up. You're now in for a night of telly. Nothing to do. Nothing to think about.

Because the seeking is over. There is nothing to do any more. Well, that's what your brain may come to realize anyway.

Whatever, it sounds attractive, doesn't it?

The message of oneness is that we are all *it* already. We are all *there* already. We don't have to go looking anywhere for the answer. Because the answer is here. You are the answer. This book is the answer. The ticking of the clock is the answer. You could call everything around you and everyone around you – all those things and people that seem separate to you – your invitation. Your invitation to see that all is one.

OK, let's rest for a minute.

If the seeking is over, you can start by giving up trying to get this all in one go.

You will find that something in you 'gets' it.

That something in you feels relief at certain things you read.

The message here speaks to the part of you that already knows this. Or rather, oneness reminds oneness that it is one.

So, just keep sitting back. Taking little sips of this wine and just enjoying the taste of it. Enjoying what's on the telly. Even enjoying the adverts. Because everything is one. Even metaphors getting mixed up is one playing at metaphors getting mixed up.

When the seeking is over, there is a beautiful sense of relief. Like the wine seeping into all parts of your being, softening and relaxing as it goes:

> *There is no seeking because this is it. It's all here already.*
>
> *There is no seeking because there is nothing to find.*
>
> *There is no seeking because there is no one there to find anything.*
>
> *The seeking is over now. All there is, is this. And this, at the moment, is the slowly percolating message of oneness.*

In Lewis Carroll's book *Through the Looking-Glass and What Alice Found There*, Alice is wandering through the woods when she comes across the Red King, asleep. She wonders what he is dreaming about. She wonders whether she is just a part of his dream. That she *herself* is in a dream. And at that moment she can see the dreamer, dreaming her, the dreamt.

You may have come across different spiritual philosophies that talk about life as a dream. Well, if all is one, then this world of separation that we apparently live in has to be a dream.

And the dream is a good metaphor because we know that within our sleeping dreams we are unaware – at the time of the dream – of the fact that it is a dream. Within the sleeping dream, we believe we are in 'reality'. It's only when we 'wake up' that we recognize that it was a dream.

This, of course, offers the possibility that the 'reality' that we 'wake up' into is itself another dream. Another dream that itself can be woken up from. Rather like a set of Russian dolls of dreams within dreams. And indeed, in this area of 'spirituality', people talk about awakening. And those who have awakened will often talk about their previous 'reality' as being just a dream.

At this point, I'd like to make a quick aside about the inverted commas that are beginning to litter the page like the fouled pavement of a suburban street. Here I am, writing (and you reading) a book full of words, when words are so difficult for this message. It goes *beyond* words. Yet, here we are, left with little but words. So those dog-shit-like inverted commas are there when the meaning of the words is straining (straining at the leash, if you want to mix up another darn metaphor).

So, please excuse the inverted turds. Let them give you a hint that our words are so grounded in dualism – in our world of twos – when what we're talking about is a world of one.

The dream, then, is oneness playing at being two and more. Oneness playing at being separate individuals and separate things. When all there is, is one.

Take another sip of wine and relax. You now know something, at least: that the seeking is over.

You realize there is nothing to do.

Like a drunk couple arm in arm, staggering the last few steps to their front door, the fact that there is nothing to do goes arm in arm with the fact that the seeking is over.

Because if we're already there – if this is it, as it is, here, and the seeking is over – of course there is nothing to do.

But try telling your mind that.

Good mind, bad mind

Let's have a few moments on the subject of the mind. The mind has received a lot of bad press in spiritual circles. It always has, really, but even more so recently with books like *The Power of Now*.

Having shaken off the mind control of religious leaders, most people's minds are now under attack from the leaders of the new spiritualities.

To be outrageously simplistic (well, it's better than being outrageously manipulative, anyway), religion is about reaffirming the dualism of the mind. So you have 'good' thoughts and feelings, and 'bad' thoughts and feelings. And you should do whatever you can to eliminate those bad ones. As an incentive, it's worth knowing that the bad ones lead you to eternal hell and damnation.

Modern spirituality seems to have shaken off the more obvious moral territories of good and bad, steering us instead towards preferred states. For example, it is better to be calm and peaceful than pissed off and angry. It is better to be still than noisy. It is better to be in the now than in the past or the future.

The mind – pesky little devil that it is – is always wandering off into the past and dwelling on things. Or it is shooting off into the future: dreaming, planning, delaying.

So the trick is to be in the present. Be present to what you are doing in the moment. This brings consciousness, and ultimately, peace.

Of course, this is fine for a few 'moments', but the mind is like a child. It will wander off. It will play. If you fancy chaining your child-mind to the chair and forcing it to eat the moment-food, then please do. But your child-mind is likely to be sick on the moment-food.

There is one interesting truism in the whole 'be in the moment' game, though, and that is the observation that the past and the future do not exist. Of course, this has to be true.

In the 'be in the moment' game, the past and the future do not exist.

The only thing that ever exists is the present. The past is in the mind, and the future is in the mind. But that doesn't make them 'wrong'.

In a world of one, everything is just fine. Because everything is one just playing at doing something. So there's no state that's better than any other state.

There's no way to think that's any better than any other way to think.

If you're thinking about that great holiday you had last year, that's fine. That's oneness playing at being a thought about last year's great holiday.

If you're worrying about the presentation you have to make to the board next week, that's fine. That's oneness playing at being a worried thought about a presentation.

This is not the same as saying that everything is 'perfect', as that worried thought certainly doesn't feel perfect.

But it actually has no more superior or inferior quality to it than any other thought.

So if no thought is better than any other thought, then you've no need to do anything to improve your thoughts.

All your thoughts are oneness thinking.

And if your mind is now going, 'OK, but I want to get this "awakening" thing; what do I need to do?', well, the answer is that there is *nothing* to do, because nothing you do will change anything.

And not doing anything won't change anything, either.

There is literally nothing to do.

It's absolutely hopeless.

So at this point your mind can start to get pissed off with the fact that it can't get that – that there's nothing for it to grab on to.

Or your mind can take another sip of wine and just vaguely like the idea of not having to do anything.

You see that all there is, is this.

Your mind should like this bit, because it's all rather nice, in a reassuring, English kind of way. This is good, solid, sturdy stuff.

There is nothing other than this.

This is arising

I'll now introduce a word that I'll use a lot from now on – 'arising'. At this apparent point in the history of the apparent world, a bunch of things are arising for you.

Your seeing of this page is arising. Your hearing of cars outside is arising. An ache in your leg is arising. A warm feeling in your lower back is arising. A thought around the content of these words is arising.

That's what I mean by 'this is it'. This – all these arisings – is it. There's nothing else. All these arisings are oneness arising. They are all nothing arising as something.

Just get a sense of it.

In the dream, we construct whole entities of self (a mind-body person with a history and a future); of others; of a world beyond our immediate experience. All is separate and individual. All has a comparative quality to it: it is hot or cold, light or dark, good or bad, big or small, helpful or unhelpful.

In the dream, everything is complicated. And the separation creates tension and conflict in every sphere. On a simple, personal level, this means that we are constantly 'dealing' with other individuals. Are they better or worse than I am? Can I get something from them? Do they want something from me? And so on.

Whereas,

This

Is

It.

There is no moral quality to anything that arises. Nothing that arises is the effect of anything else. Nothing that arises will be the cause of anything else. All that arises is one just arising.

Let's take some examples that we can relate to, and see how this works. I've tried to use people and situations that are likely to resonate with you – people like you, living lives like yours.

Esther is a small old woman who lives on a small sheep farm on a small island in Scotland's Outer Hebrides. Her life is hard. She lived through a joyless and childless marriage to Jack. Then he was found one morning – his bones crushed – at the bottom of a cliff, under a tractor. What made his death all the more painful was that the tractor was not his. He'd stolen it from a nearby farm and was recklessly joyriding in the early hours.

So, Esther is alone with her sheep and her difficult memories. And life is hard in this place called the Outer Hebrides. The Inner Hebrides are windy, cold and difficult, even for the sheep that live there, so imagine what the Outer Hebrides are like.

It is a bright April morning. That's not to say it's warm, but the sun is out and as Esther hangs her Monday wash on the line, she can see across the rugged moorland out to sea.

So, Esther has a story. She has a past (grim). She has a present. And she has a future (grim). But as she hangs out her washing, this is what arises for her:

* The feeling of coldness in her hands.
* The thought that her hands are cold.
* The thought of a warm cup of tea.
* An ache in her back.
* The smell of the sea.
* The sound of gulls.

* The memory of a childhood holiday in Inverness.

* The memory of the smell of her dad's aftershave.

* Sadness that her dad has gone.

* Sadness that her husband has gone.

* The thought of a warm cup of tea.

And this – for 'Esther' – is it. There is nothing else around these arisings. The fiction – the dream – is that there is more around this. That there are other bits of history. That there are other pains. That there is more sadness, and that sadness is not good. That there is a body and a mind called Esther.

All this is the fiction that surrounds simply what is. And what is, is the arising at any one time.

Let's hear a more dramatic story.

Philip was diagnosed with lung cancer one month ago, and the prognosis is not good. Since then, his life has swirled around him like water slowly disappearing down a plughole. Everything looks different. His important job in a merchant bank in the City of London seems utterly unimportant. The noise his two young children make when they are playing – a sound that so recently had grated on his nerves – pulls at his heart. And the devoted wife he took for granted for so long is now achingly appreciated.

For Philip, life is now pain. The physical pain and discomfort of the cancer and the treatment for it. And, more than this, the emotional pain. The pain of mortality being faced, and the prospect of losing everything in his life. It is all too painful. He wonders about his past, about all that he took for granted. He mourns his lost future.

He watches his six-year-old son playing and the tears flow.

He hears his four-year-old daughter laughing in another room and his heart aches.

For Philip, the stakes are higher. Everything is more intense. The 'story' of his life is more real and more potent than for most of us.

But for Philip, too, this story is no less of a fiction. A fiction surrounding the is-ness of what is.

Philip returned from his chemotherapy session at the hospital two hours ago. He is now lying on the lounge sofa, watching the early evening news on the television. This is what arises for him:

*   A feeling of sickness in his belly.

*   The hearing of pots being clanked around in the kitchen.

*   The memory of his mother cooking for him.

*   The thought of his children missing him.

*   The feeling of sadness.

*   The feeling of sickness.

*   The seeing of a healthy-looking news presenter – all pristine.

*   The thought of the unfairness of it all.

*   The feeling of sickness.

This is what arises in that instant. This is all that there is. Without the judgement of it, there is just a feeling of sickness. Or a feeling of sadness.

And that's it. What surrounds 'what is' here is the fiction, the dream, the story.

No matter what colour we give each story, or each bunch of arisings, it doesn't alter the fact that all there is, is this.

You find that everything is appropriate (not perfect).

Everything is...

A few years back, a friend of mine was heavily into a few 'spiritual' ideas, one of which was that 'everything is just perfect'. I'm sure you've heard this before. Like many spiritual ideas, it sprouts from the best of intentions and has some root of truth poking out of it.

It wraps up a few apparent truisms. The first is that we can't do much better than to accept most things just as they are. This is good practice: most people waste inordinate amounts of time and energy resisting what so obviously is. They complain about what they can't change; they get upset about people who won't change; and they take personally what wasn't personal. In many senses, the non-acceptance of the unchangeable is dysfunctional.

The second apparent truism is that if we think positively we tend to attract positive stuff into our lives. And this seems to work. If we go out with a smile on our face, people tend to respond better to us. That seems to expand into a whole life philosophy. When we are positive, the world seems to respond positively. Or, as my friend would say frequently, the 'universe' responds positively. What? Did the stars smile back? The universe, my goodness me.

For my friend, everything, apparently, was perfect. When we missed the bus and had to stand in the rain for 20 minutes, it was perfect. When our football team got relegated, it was perfect. When I picked up some virus and ended up in the hospital for two weeks, it was perfect. It used to drive me potty. It's not bloody perfect, I'd say, it's bloody crap. We've missed the bloody bus. That is in no way perfect. And then, as if to reinforce my own negative patterns, a car would drive by through a puddle and soak me.

> *Life can be very good, and then it can be very shit.*

Life is not perfect. That's the point. Life is the perfect mix of great and shit. The ups are invariably followed by the downs. Happiness is invariably followed by a bit of a downer. Life can be very good, and then it can be very shit. Or it can drag along feeling OK, then turn the corner of OK and just feel vaguely dissatisfying.

But the fact that life is like this is great news, because the fact that it goes round and round – from great to shit, and from 'good' to 'bad' – and that the world is as jam-packed with bad people as it is good, reminds us that it's an ingeniously created dream.

Just as trying to be in the 'now' might work for a few consecutive nows, but then be trampled over by the wonderful child-mind, so positive thinking and accepting everything thinking is trampled over by the negative thought and the pissed-off-with-everything thought.

And, again, it's not that the mind is the culprit here.

If everything is one, then everything is OK – all the thoughts, all the bits and pieces, they're all OK. Because they're all one playing the game of being two.

So, when we say everything is perfect, it simply doesn't work. We say it within the context of the dream, where everything certainly isn't perfect.

But when the dream is seen for what it is – apparently good bits perfectly balanced by apparently bad bits, but all in actuality exactly the same (one) thing – it is seen that everything is simply OK.

Everything is the same as everything else because it is literally the same thing.

So, if you fancy nailing some spiritual aphorism to your sleeve, have a go at 'Everything is OK' or 'Everything is appropriate'.

It's OK, it's not real

OK, we've fixed up a one-to-one session with God for you. And He's got some good news:

'My child, you are safe. Nothing can happen to you now. You are in my arms. Just relax and fall back in the knowledge that everything is OK now.'

Thank you, God, very good.

And this is a message that God has been giving people for a good long time. Except, when we're stuck in the dream, yet again, the words seem to wear a bit thin in the face of 'experience'.

Outside the dream, there is something to this idea of being 'safe'.

Remember, if there is just one arising as individuals, then individuals do not really exist. There is no you. You do not exist. (OK, yes, fill up the glass again.)

You do not exist. There is no you. There is no life. There is no point. There is nothing to gain. And nothing to lose.

This is dreadful, of course. But can you feel any relief in there, too?

Ironically, there is always a dual response to the full message of oneness. At once, it's the last thing we want to hear and the thing we've been searching for.

It's certainly the last thing we want to hear:

I do not exist? My achievements do not exist? My hopes amount to nothing? My life is a fiction, a dream? I cannot make a difference? I have no choice?

And it's what we crave, too.

If there is no point, then there is no struggle for meaning.

If there is no me, then there is no tension with the other(s).

If I can't make a difference, then I don't have to try.

If nothing can happen to 'me', then I am SAFE.

Of course, there is no 'safe' or 'unsafe'; there just is this.

But there is something in the dreamer that feels a sense of safety as the dream (and dreamer) begins to dissolve into the sand.

The Daleks have been building up to this for weeks. They've finally cornered Doctor Who in the corner of a bunker. Exterminate. Exterminate. Exterminate. You cower behind the sofa, peeking at the TV through your fingers.

Pause.

An aside here. This scene has become a cliché. It's been shared and mentioned and referred to so many times now (when you were drunk as a student; in TV programmes, etc). But are any of us sure that it's an 'actual' memory, rather than just a shared and fictionalized memory?

I for one am not sure whether I did actually cower behind the sofa. I may have been standing there in my blue Adidas tracksuit, pointing and saying to my parents: 'Have you seen this garbage, parents? They expect children to suspend their disbelief at the sight of some squeaking robots made out of the rubbish from the back of the *Blue Peter* studio. This is gutter TV. Opium for the mini masses. Mind-sedation drugs injected straight into the carotid artery of today's pre-teen youth.'

My parents would then peek out from behind the sofa and say, 'Yes, darling… argghhh, no, they're coming, quick hide.' But here we are again. 'Reality' crumbles at the slightest push.

OK, let's hit the play button again.

For the sake of this (elongated) point, you're behind the sofa, scared. What does your mum *really* say at times like this? 'It's OK, love, it's only made-up. They're just actors in costumes.' And you feel better.

And it still happens. When a scene in a film is too painful, we remind ourselves that it's just a film. That these are actors. That this is probably their tenth take, and there's a whole crew behind the camera. (I felt this recently while watching Clint Eastwood's *Million Dollar Baby*.)

It's a film. It's not real. And we feel better.

Well, this is a dream. It's not real.

You don't exist.

Now feel better darn it, FEEL BETTER.

5

THE
F**K IT
FORM

Saying F**k It is enough to sort anyone out (it is, after all, the Ultimate Spiritual Way). Relaxing deeply and letting go can resolve any problem. The simple act of relaxing is more powerful than any form of yoga or Tai Chi. The truth is, though, that our minds like a bit of form: something to get stuck into, to learn and remind us that we're doing ourselves good. So welcome to The F**k It Form. The form without form.

The F**k It Form takes postures from life (such as being slumped on the settee watching telly), adjusts them slightly, adds a dash of consciousness (awareness of what you're doing) and a dollop-full of relaxation, and gives you a great form that will do you a lot of good. Indeed, the precise benefits of each posture are given here, so you've plenty to chew on.

THE ROOTS OF THE F**K IT FORM

The F**k It Form is a form of Chi Kung. Just as Tai Chi is a form of Chi Kung. Let me explain. Chi Kung is the Chinese energy practice. In fact, it literally means 'practice with energy'. And this means that any time you consciously work with your energy, you are doing Chi Kung. If you sit there now, reading this book, and relax your body and imagine the *chi* flowing through your hands, then you are doing Chi Kung.

That's what I love about it. You don't have to go to classes, you don't have to read any books, you don't have to learn any complicated forms, you can just do Chi Kung wherever you are. I mean, you can do all those other things if you want: I went to classes for years, read dozens of books, learned many complicated forms, so help yourself if that's what you fancy. But you won't get anywhere any faster by doing those things. In fact, I guarantee that you'll experience more energy sooner doing The F**k It Form than by learning Tai Chi.

And, yes, Tai Chi is a form of Chi Kung, too. It's probably the most famous form. It is a typical Chi Kung moving form: the movements are very slow, and they are designed to exercise different energy systems of the body. The problem, though, with a form like Tai Chi, is that it takes such a very long time to learn properly. It can take a couple of years to learn the basic moves. And that's before you start to learn the deep energetic work. I love Tai Chi, and I'm glad I put in the hours because I don't think I could be bothered nowadays.

The F**k It Form: expend little effort and get maximum results.

The F**k It Form is for those who want to feel the benefits of Chi Kung, but without the effort. And – by the way – that is very much the Taoist way: to expend little effort and get maximum results.

So here's the form that requires the least effort: the form that says F**k It to Form. Like Tai Chi, if you do the whole form, you'll give your whole energy system a thorough cleansing.

If you do this form every day for a month, you'll notice profound benefits: you will feel considerably more relaxed all of the time, you will sleep better, your appetite will stabilize and you'll begin to heal any illness.

Like anything of a F**k It nature, don't take it too seriously, and don't attach yourself to any of these predicted benefits. Do it because you like the feeling of energy in your body, and because you are one of the first to practise a new world-wide energetic form.

Practice

The whole idea of the F**k It Form is that you can do it as part of your normal day. Each position is based on something that you already do. So all you have to do is make a tiny adjustment to your position (such as making sure your feet are parallel, or your knees are slightly bent), breathe consciously and become aware of your *chi*, and – hey, presto – you're doing The F**k It Form.

So daily practice is important if you want to start building up your *chi*. If you can't even manage a little practice in a day, you lazy dog, then say F**k It and just try it tomorrow.

Breathing

Breathing is vital for all the postures and movements. Otherwise you'll die. And we don't want any deaths, do we now?

It's worth starting to play with belly-breathing in the F**k It Form. Belly-breathing? Yes, breathing into your belly, old chap. If you watch a baby breathing, you'll notice that the first thing that happens when he breathes in is that his belly inflates. And as he breathes out, his belly deflates. This is the natural way of breathing.

For one reason or another, at some point in our childhood (probably when we got very scared about something) we began to breathe mainly into our chests. So if you observe most adults breathing, their chests will rise as they breathe in and fall as they breathe out. And not a lot will be happening in their bellies. This way of breathing can be very good for emergencies, but it isn't so good for normal life. It's a shallow breath – and shallow breath means shallow life.

If you want to live more deeply, you have to breathe more deeply. And that means getting the breath down into your belly. So try it now: as you breathe in, push out the muscles of your belly. Imagine there is a balloon in your belly and you have to inflate the balloon with each inbreath. And then deflate the balloon with each outbreath.

> *If you want to live more deeply, you have to breathe more deeply.*

Just learning how to breathe like this can change your life. Just changing from a chest (shallow) breather to a belly (deep) breather can have tremendous physiological effects. You're filling your lungs more effectively (with a chest breath you will never fill more than two-thirds of your lungs), so you're getting more oxygen (the main fuel for your body).

The new action of your diaphragm (it pushes down deeply on the inbreath rather than lifting up slightly) creates a tremendous massage for all your internal organs. The massaged organs get a rush of blood, which is as welcome as a warm shower. The whole intestinal system gets a good massage, too, allowing it to more effectively give your body what it needs and get rid of the stuff that it doesn't.

The other great thing about belly-breathing is that you have to discard some vanity (shallow), as with really good belly-breathing your belly will puff out to the size of Buddha's (and he has a great belly). You can replace some of this vanity with acceptance (deep), and enjoy the feeling of health and relaxation that this breathing brings.

You may also need to discard belts that have fixed positions in favour of something more elastic, so everything can move more fluidly down there.

How *chi* develops

The more you consciously work with your *chi*, the more *chi* will develop in your body. Imagine that every day of conscious practice with *chi* is like putting a pound coin into a jar. Over time it really builds up. Only this jar is managed by one hell of an investment manager. At the moment he's managing to get a 200 per cent return on your investment. And, given that you're reinvesting all the profit and the holdings are giving you an extra yearly dividend, you're doing rather well. Just imagine how rich you'll be after just a few years. That's how *chi* works.

The more you consciously work with chi, *the more* chi *will develop in your body.*

And this is how *chi* works in the moment. The Chinese say: 'First the mind. Then the *chi*. Then the blood.' (Only they say it in Chinese because it would be weird otherwise.) It's succinct but true.

When you think about a part of your body, say, the palm of your hand, then *chi* will begin to flow there. And once the *chi* starts to flow, then blood will follow it.

That's why *chi* practice (Chi Kung) is so powerful: you get all the benefits of balancing the energy system and you get the accompanying physical benefits of blood flow, too.

RECLINED SITTING POSTURES

Holding the goose's egg

To get into this basic sofa posture, slump on the sofa as if you're watching the telly. In fact, watch the telly if you want. Make sure your feet are flat on the floor and positioned shoulder-width apart (that is, the outside of your feet should be the same distance apart as from the edge of one shoulder to the other), your spine is relaxed and your head facing forwards (not up). Relax your jaw and place the tip of your tongue on the roof of your mouth, just behind the upper teeth.

Now place your hands on your belly, one over the other. If you're a man, you should place the left hand against your belly first, then place the right hand relaxedly on top of it. If you're a woman, place the right hand against the belly first. The bottom hand should be positioned so that the base of the thumb rests comfortably against the belly button.

Now breathe slowly into this position. Start to feel the *chi* circulating.

The Benefits of This Posture

In this posture you are directing *chi* into the *dan tien*, the primary energy storage point in the body. This creates a general tonic for the body and is the base exercise that all other F**k It Form exercises should be built upon. If you're going to do only one exercise, then do this one. It nourishes the kidneys, so it will help calm you down and reduce anxiety.

Peacock fans its wings

Get into the basic sofa posture (as before). Now clasp your hands behind your head, placing your thumbs just beneath the occiput, the bony ridge at the bottom of the skull. Use your thumbs to massage this area. Now breathe slowly into this position. Start to feel the *chi* circulating.

The Benefits of This Posture

The stretching of the arms tonifies the heart meridian – so you will feel happier within just the first minute. Pushing back the shoulders also opens your lungs, promoting deeper breathing and the releasing of any stagnant *chi*. Massaging the occiput stimulates the acupuncture point *Fengchi* – great for reducing symptoms of stress, including headaches and eye problems.

Holding the sacred bow

Get into the basic sofa posture (as before). Cross your left leg over the right, so that the left ankle rests gently on the top of the thigh of the right leg. Now grasp the ankle of the left leg with your right hand. Let your left hand simply fall onto the cushion beside you, palm facing upwards. Now breathe slowly into this position. Start to feel the *chi* circulating. When you have felt the full benefits of this position, change legs.

The Benefits of This Posture

The gentle stretch shifts stagnant energy in the legs, so it's a good tonic for restless, tired legs. The gallbladder meridian and yin channels of the legs are stretched, affecting your clarity and creativity. So if you want clarity in any situation – or to get an idea for something – get into this posture. Pulling the ankle farther up towards the groin will increase the benefits.

Slain by dragon fire

Get into the basic sofa posture (as before). Now simply let your arms drop to your sides, palms facing up. Imagine that you have indeed been slain by a dragon, and that you are now lying lifeless in the position in which you were slain. Feel the weight of your lifeless body on the sofa. It's a great position with which to end the first sequence, just as death is a good way to end the sequence of life.

Imagine now that the dragon is still there and still breathing fire on you. Imagine that the fire is very precisely directed. First, the dragon is directing the fire at your heart. Feel the heat and the power entering your heart. The dragon then directs the fire into your solar plexus. Feel the heat and power entering this tender point. And last, the dragon directs fire into your belly, your *dan tien*. Feel the heat and power entering your *dan tien*, the primary energy centre of your whole being.

The Benefits of This Posture

The initial posture allows the *chi* to sink in your body. This will make you feel more grounded. You will instantly feel calmer, less fearful and be ready to embrace life, not be scared of it.

The fire of the dragon is a very powerful healing technique. The energy enters your body and goes to wherever it is needed, as well as the point it entered. So your heart will benefit (joy), your solar plexus will benefit (openness) and your *dan tien* will benefit (centredness and energy). Then the energy moves to any area of energy imbalance in your body.

In Chinese Medicine, these three areas relate to the Triple Burner – which you need to clear to create a balanced flow of energy through the body. As you do the exercise, you may well start to feel a spiralling of energy down through your body.

UPRIGHT SITTING POSTURES

Golden hands

Get into the basic sitting posture: sit in any chair where your back can be upright and your feet can rest flat on the floor. Make sure your feet are a few inches apart and that they are parallel to each other (i.e., so that your feet are neither toe-out nor toe-in). Feel that you're sitting comfortably on your sitting bones, without any support from the back of the chair. Imagine a golden thread attached to the crown of your head that lifts your head up and straightens the spine. The pulling golden thread will also have the effect of dropping your chin slightly.

Be aware that there are two directional forces at work in your body. Imagine a coat hanger on a rail. And on the coat hanger hangs a silk dress. Your skeleton is the coat hanger. And just as the coat hanger is being suspended by the hook on the rail (an upward force), you are being suspended by the golden thread (an upward force).

Everything else in your body can be like the silk dress – just hanging from the solid support of the coat hanger (a downward force). So all your muscles, skin, organs, the whole gooey lot of you can simply sink towards the ground (a downward force). Really feel the sensation of letting yourself sink towards the ground. Last, place the tip of your tongue lightly on the roof of your mouth, just behind the upper teeth.

That's the sitting posture. You now simply do different things with your hands.

For golden hands, let your arms just dangle by your sides. So from your shoulders down, there should be no intervention from your muscles whatsoever. Now breathe slowly into this position. And begin to feel the chi collecting in your hands. This is the gold of chi being generated: thus, golden hands.

The Benefits of This Posture

Lengthening the spine like this opens up the governing *du* channel, helping us stay alert and full of energy. The rising *chi* invigorates the whole body, whilst the mind calms down.

You'll feel the strong *chi* collecting in your hands, and this will also boost your circulation.

You can also increase the benefit to your kidneys by rubbing your *chi*-full hands on them before you move on to the next posture.

Monkey scratches back

Get into the sitting posture (as before). With your left hand resting in your lap, take your right hand over your right shoulder, as if you're going to scratch your back. In fact, you can begin to rub your back with your fingers. Make sure that you rub either side of the spine: maybe with your first finger on one side of the spine and your index finger on the other side.

Relax and breathe into this position. You can either continue to rub the spine or just rest your hand on your back. Once you can feel the *chi* flowing and you're ready to move on, simply do the same with your left hand.

The Benefits of This Posture

This position stretches the heart meridian, settles your mind and allows you to massage the bladder meridian. This ultimately supports the vital kidney energy system, and helps strengthen the whole of your back. Not bad for a little rub.

Tiger's paws

Get into the sitting posture (as before). Now simply let your hands rest in your lap with the palms facing upwards. Make sure your arms are completely relaxed. Just let your hands rest there. Breathe slowly into this posture. You will begin to feel *chi* flowing into the palms of your hands, making them feel tingly, soft and tender, like the soft paws of a tiger.

The Benefits of This Posture

You can sit in this posture for a long time. It is a great meditation position. Your mind will calm down and stressful thoughts will disappear. The focus on the breath strengthens the lungs and boosts *chi* in the whole body. The focus on the palms stimulates the crucial point *Laogong*. You can even try breathing through your palms: sucking in *chi* on the inbreath through these *chi* gateways, and releasing stagnant *chi* on the outbreath. Or if you prefer to keep it simple, sit there quietly and you'll notice your cold hands become warm.

STANDING POSTURES

The resting warrior

All these standing postures are great to do when you're waiting for something. Whether it's a Tube train or a bus, or for your mate to turn up at the pub, these are perfect to get into any time you're standing around.

So, first get into the basic standing posture. Your feet should be shoulder-width apart – that is, the outside edges of your feet should be the same distance apart as your shoulders. Make sure your feet are parallel to each other, neither toe-out nor toe-in. If you want to be very precise about this, if you drew a line from the middle (the bi-section) of your heel under your foot to the middle (the bi-section) of your toes, then these are the lines that you want to be getting parallel.

Your knees should be slightly bent. The more you bend your knees, the more *chi* you'll generate, but the more difficult it is to stand for a while. So, at first, just bend your knees slightly.

Next, you need to 'tuck your tail in'. To get the feeling of what this means, stick your bum out, then do the opposite: push your bum in. This is tucking your tail in. It feels weird at first, but like the whole posture, you'll get used to it after a bit. Standing like this, with your tail tucked in, feels like perching on the edge of a bar stool. The physical effect of standing like this is to straighten your spine and allow the full belly-breathing to work.

Up we go now to the head, where you want to imagine the golden thread suspending your head from the crown. This will allow you to relax and drop your jaw slightly. Last, allow the tip of your tongue to lightly touch the roof of your mouth, just behind your upper teeth.

Although this may seem like a rather complicated and weird routine to go through just to stand up, you'll get the hang of it very quickly, and each pointer has a very important reason for it (which I won't go into now at the risk of you thinking it's even more complicated than you do already). You just have to trust me on this one.

Standing like this, you are practically in the resting warrior. All you have to do now is put your hands in your trouser pockets. If you don't have any pockets, pretend you have and just rest your palms against your body.

Now just rest in this posture. Breathe slowly and deeply. And – given this posture will feel pretty peculiar – just keep bringing your attention to the bits of you that start to feel uncomfortable and simply relax them. The main thing with a posture like this – at the beginning – is to keep going… just keep relaxing. I hope the Tube or the bus or your mate take a few more minutes, because it's really good to stand like this for a while to get to feel the relaxation that comes from going through tension again and again.

The Benefits of This Posture

This posture – like all the standing postures – provides a great general tonic to the energy system. That's why they're at the heart of most Chi Kung practices. After just a short amount of practice you will feel deeply calm in a way that can last for the day (or at least the Tube/bus journey or time with your mate).

Warming the heavenly globe

Get into the standing posture (as before). Now simply place your hands in your jacket pockets. If you're not wearing a jacket, or a top with pockets in, just imagine you are, placing your hands over your belly, on either side of your belly button.

Now breathe deeply into your belly and feel the *chi* beginning to accumulate there. You'll feel this largely as a sensation of increasing warmth in your belly, under your hands. The heavenly globe is the *dan tien*, the seat of your energy system. And with this posture you are, indeed, warming it.

This is one of my favourite postures. I buy jumpers and tops with pockets over the belly just so that I can do it whenever I'm out and about.

The Benefits of This Posture

Your mind will calm down and stressful thoughts will disappear. You will strengthen the *chi* in your *dan tien* (remember, that's the engine-room of your energy system). This will help clear stagnation of blood in the body – which is particularly good for menstrual and reproductive function in women. And if – chaps – this has made you angry (you want your benefits, too, of course), then remember that this exercise also stimulates liver *chi*, which will calm down any anger.

Receiving a multitude of gifts

Get into the standing posture (as before). Let your arms dangle by your sides. Then allow your palms to face forwards. Keep your arms and hands relaxed. As you breathe, you'll feel the *chi* flowing into your hands. This pose opens you to the energy of the Earth and heavens. Receive whatever gifts come your way: relaxation, inspiration, healing.

The Benefits of This Posture

This can be the most surprising of all postures. You may feel something different every time. You may feel different sensations and experience different states of mind. It is the most open of postures, so you open to whatever you need at that time. Just be open and wait for your multitude of gifts.

The owl

Get into the standing posture (as before). Clasp your hands together behind your back: one hand holding the other and the thumbs interlocking. You will no doubt see (contented-looking) old people standing and walking in this position. And it is, indeed, a key to a long life. I love to stand and stare at good views or bad people in this posture. And when I wander around like this, I feel instantly calm.

The Benefits of This Posture

Your arms are cradling your kidneys, so this is very nourishing for the kidney energy system. The kidneys, remember, are the vital essence of the body – so nourishing them is a very good idea. The stretch on the arms boosts the yang meridians, so helping to warm the body.

Everything about this posture is calming and soothing.

MOVING POSTURES

Ascending the white mountains

This posture is known in the West as cleaning your teeth. Cleaning your teeth mindfully is a truly beautiful exercise. Mainly because we so rarely think about this twice-daily activity. We just get on and do it, thinking only about what we have to do afterwards.

So it can be a beautiful exercise in mindfulness and consciousness. Treat it as you would any F**k It Form posture: make sure your knees are bent, check that you're fully relaxed, focus on the breathing. Then really feel what it's like to clean your teeth. Notice the taste of the toothpaste, how the brush feels on your gums, what your tongue is up to whilst all this is going on.

The Benefits of This Posture

Your dental hygiene levels will improve instantly, as you will clean your teeth more thoroughly and carefully. Change to a toothpaste containing peppermint and you'll magnify the benefits, as this stimulates *chi* in the body. The stomach meridian is stimulated: so look after your teeth and you're looking after your stomach. If you chomp your teeth together occasionally, you'll also stimulate the vital kidney system – the first victim of stress and tiredness.

Diving in shallow lake

Known in the West as doing the washing-up. As in ascending the white mountains, diving in shallow lake is a beautiful exercise in mindfulness. While cleaning your teeth is a quick, unconsidered action, doing the washing-up is a more drawn-out, and usually painful, affair. We tend to do it as fast as we can while distracting ourselves as effectively as possible (e.g., with a radio), and look forward to the whole hideous episode being over smartish. Which is why it's so good to get 'mindful' around it.

Mindfulness is all about bringing your attention to what you're doing. Rather than trying to get out of focusing on what you're doing, you deliberately keep bringing your attention back to it. You bring your attention into the present moment (when it's normally in the past or future) and into the present space and activity (when it's usually wandering around somewhere else entirely).

And I'm not the first to enter the bubbly and rubber-gloved world of washing-up as an exercise for mindfulness and meditation. The Buddhists have been chopping wood, carrying water and washing pots for millennia.

So, use your experience of the F**k It still meditation forms to relax into a good posture, and get washing. Keep relaxing your legs and arms. Then bring your attention to what it's really like to wash pots: notice how the warm water feels (apart from warm, smart-arse), the sounds of the pots as they touch each other, the beauty of light reflecting in the washing-up bubbles.

It may be difficult to contain yourself after a couple of gos at this exercise. You'll start volunteering to do the washing-up at every possible opportunity. This will give you many points with partners, friends and relatives, but it may give you slightly rougher-looking hands, so remember to use a good moisturizer, folks.

The Benefits of This Posture

The mindfulness you learn in this exercise will most probably seep into the rest of your life: the shift in your perception and state of mind can be enormous and life-changing.

Simply putting your hands in warm water creates a lot of *chi* flow in the vital meridians along the arms and running into each of the fingers. These include the heart meridian (you'll feel happier), the pericardium meridian (you'll feel more open) and the lung meridian (you'll feel more free).

Wow, they should charge for letting you do the washing-up, really.

THE POST-COITAL SMOKE

IT WAS GOOD FOR ME

Yes, thank you very much. This intimate experience with you is nearly over. But I've enjoyed it. It was good for me. And that's just about all that matters (though my publisher won't agree with that, of course). The truth is that when we do what we fancy (bar serial murdering-like activities), we not only please ourselves, but others, too. In the end we all want to do just what the hell we please. And those who are living their lives like this tend to inspire us (or really piss us off if we're particularly uptight).

This is the essence of F**k It. To spit in the face of obligation, expectation, rules and regulations. To Say F**k It and go your own way.

So please (soon) close this book and go your own way.

WHY F**K IT IS THE ULTIMATE SPIRITUAL WAY (just in case you haven't been paying attention and want something easy to say in the pub)

Life is spiritual. Life just flows. Life doesn't judge or criticize. Life doesn't resist what is. Because life *is* what is.

Life is pure softness and relaxation. Resistance to life is hardness and tension.

F**k It is the movement from tension (in whatever form) to relaxation (in every form).

F**k It is a most profane way of saying the most profound thing: that when we relax and give in to the simple flow of life, we will experience the ultimate freedom.

Say, 'Life is life, man,' then 'I love you, mate, I really love you.'

So F**k It is The Ultimate Spiritual Way.

(OK, so it's not going to be that easy to say in the pub… but just slur the words a bit and say, 'Life is life, man,' then 'I love you, mate, I really love you,' and you will have just about hit the nail on the head.)

I'D LIKE TO SEE YOU AGAIN SOMETIME (if that's OK with you)

Yes, I've enjoyed myself and I'd love to see you again sometime. We get on, don't you think? So let's do it again.

As a loose arrangement (and please feel free to suggest something else if you fancy), I thought we could meet in the bookshop, just like last time. I'll have lots more interesting things to share.

Sure, I was a little put out when you took me into the loo so soon, but I felt better when you took me to bed (on the first night, too, I say).

So, until next time, good night and God/Buddha/Lao Tsu/Lakshmi bless.

ABOUT THE AUTHOR

John C. Parkin is the UK's bestselling wisdom teacher.

The son of Anglican preachers, John realized that saying F**k It was as powerful as all the Eastern spiritual practices he'd been studying for 20 years. Having said F**k It to a top job in London, he escaped to Italy with his wife, Gaia, and their twin boys, where they now teach their famous F**k It Retreats in various spectacular locations (such as on the volcano of Stromboli). He spends his days spreading the F**k It message – on the retreats, in F**k It eCourses and even with F**k It Music – then says F**k It himself and naps by the pool.

wwwthefuckitlifecom

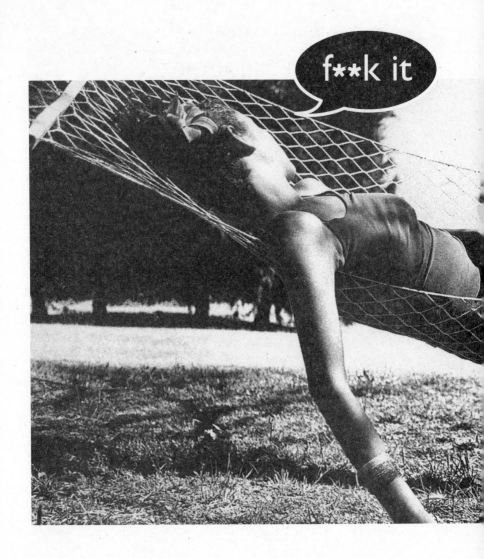

YOU'VE READ THE BOOK — NOW GO ON A F**K IT RETREAT IN ITALY

This is where it all started: John and Gaia ran their first F**k It Retreat in 2005.
They're now running these famous retreats in spectacular locations around Italy,
including an estate and spa in Urbino, and on the volcano of Stromboli.
Say F**k It and treat yourself to a F**k It Retreat.

'Anything that helps you let go is okay on a F**k It Retreat.' THE OBSERVER
'I witnessed some remarkable transformations during my F**k It Retreat.' KINDRED SPIRIT

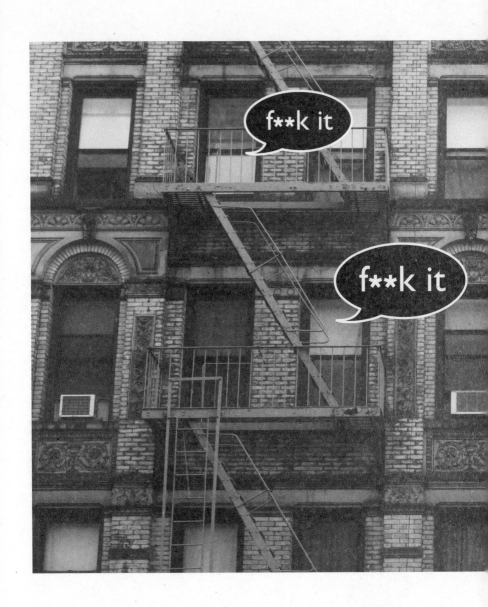

YOU'VE READ THE BOOK — NOW TRY A F**K IT ONLINE COURSE
and explore John & Gaia's teaching from anywhere in the world.

Hay House Titles of Related Interest

We hope you enjoyed this Hay House book. If you'd like to receive our online catalog featuring additional information on Hay House books and products, or if you'd like to find out more about the Hay Foundation, please contact:

Hay House, Inc., P.O. Box 5100, Carlsbad, CA 92018-5100
(760) 431-7695 or (800) 654-5126
(760) 431-6948 (fax) or (800) 650-5115 (fax)
www.hayhouse.com® • *www.hayfoundation.org*

***

Published and distributed in Australia by: Hay House Australia Pty. Ltd.,
18/36 Ralph St., Alexandria NSW 2015 • Phone: 612-9669-4299
Fax: 612-9669-4144 • www.hayhouse.com.au

Published and distributed in the United Kingdom by: Hay House UK, Ltd.,
Astley House, 33 Notting Hill Gate, London W11 3JQ
Phone: 44-20-3675-2450 • Fax: 44-20-3675-2451 • www.hayhouse.co.uk

Published and distributed in the Republic of South Africa by:
Hay House SA (Pty), Ltd., P.O. Box 990, Witkoppen 2068
Phone/Fax: 27-11-467-8904 • www.hayhouse.co.za

Published in India by: Hay House Publishers India,
Muskaan Complex, Plot No. 3, B-2, Vasant Kunj, New Delhi 110 070
Phone: 91-11-4176-1620 • Fax: 91-11-4176-1630 • www.hayhouse.co.in

Distributed in Canada by: Raincoast Books, 2440 Viking Way, Richmond, B.C. V6V 1N2
Phone: 1-800-663-5714 • Fax: 1-800-565-3770 • www.raincoast.com

***

Take Your Soul on a Vacation

Visit www.HealYourLife.com® to regroup, recharge, and reconnect
with your own magnificence.
Featuring blogs, mind-body-spirit news, and life-changing wisdom
from Louise Hay and friends.

Visit www.HealYourLife.com today!